HOW

do they get a model ship in a bottle?

HOW

do they get a model ship in a bottle?

Contents

Q How do they get a model ship in a bottle?

A You ask very nicely and tell it to suck in its gut, of course. People have been putting stuff in empty bottles for centuries. Before ships caught on, "patience bottles" were filled with scenes of religious imagery (Jesus on the cross, for example), and aptly named "mining bottles" had multilevel scenes of ore mining. The earliest mining bottle, which dates to 1719, was created by Matthias Buchinger, a well-known entertainer of the time who had no arms or legs. Mining bottles originated in what is now Hungary.

People started shoving ships into bottles in the mid- to late eighteenth century. Most people did not write the dates on their creations, and since many were made with old bottles that had been sitting around, the date on the actual bottle doesn't necessarily mean that's when the ship was put in it. The earliest ship in a bottle that someone bothered to date (on the sails) was constructed in 1784. Bottling ships really caught on in the 1830s, when clear glass became more common. It is still a popular hobby these days, with clubs and associations around the world devoted to the skill.

But how do you get that boat into the bottle? It's actually pretty simple (not easy, but simple). The hull (or bottom of the boat) is narrow enough to fit through the neck of the bottle. The masts are hinged so that they can be pushed flat against the hull. While the ship is outside the bottle, the sails are attached and a string is tied to the mast. The masts and sails are bent so that they are flat, and then the whole thing is pushed through the bottleneck. Glue or putty on the bottom of the bottle keeps the ship anchored. Once the ship is in, a long tool, shaped like a rod or skewer, is used to position it. Finally, the string that is attached to the masts is pulled to bring up the sails and complete the illusion.

There are some types of boats—motorboats, for example—that are too wide to get into the bottle in one piece. These are assembled inside the bottle using rods, which takes a lot of patience and a steady hand.

Getting a ship out of a bottle? Easy—navigate it toward an iceberg or a jagged rock.

Q How do generations get their names?

 In The Who's 1965 song "My Generation," lead singer Roger Daltrey famously declared that he hoped he'd die before he got old. But what exactly was Daltrey's generation? For starters, it didn't die; it got old, giving us, among other mediocrities, minivans along the way. We know the people from this generation as Baby Boomers.

Agreeing on a name for a generation is tricky business. Equally tricky is figuring out exactly who belongs to which generation. (There is no official Council of Generation Naming.) If it's a problem, though, it's a fairly recent one. It is only with the rise of *en masse* self-consciousness—and rampant narcissism—that people have even cared about naming generations.

Historically, generations have gotten their names from literary sources. One of the first generations to name itself was the Generation of '98, a movement of Spanish artists and writers who pointed to the Spanish-American War of 1898 as a break from an artistic and political past. The generational term Baby Boomer was coined in a 1974 *Time* magazine article about Bob Dylan. And Generation X, though around for some time beforehand, was cemented in the popular mind by Douglas Coupland's eponymous 1991 novel.

Possibly the most famous and influential—and certainly the most romantic—generation of the twentieth century was known as the Lost Generation. The term is attributed to writer Gertrude Stein, who used it to describe disillusioned World War I veterans. Stein's cohorts in Paris, among them Ernest Hemingway, embraced the term. Of course, critics are quick to point out that a few artists and expatriates traipsing about the Left Bank hardly qualify as an entire generation. Which points to the futility of such an exercise in generalization in the first place.

Historians William Strauss and Neil Howe created an entire history around generational movements. Naturally, they made an effort to name some generations themselves. (Some of their names include the rather inspired 13th Generation for the group everybody else calls Generation X, and the silly Homeland Generation for the current generational crop.) As of late, the desire for satisfactory generation names has reached a fevered pitch, with no fewer than five monikers being bandied about for the current generation. (Thankfully, it appears Howe and Strauss's Homeland Generation is gaining little traction.)

As we said, most generations have been anointed by literary critics, writers, and other intellectual types. So it is perhaps bleak testimony to the era we live in that Generation Y—the most widely recognized term for the generation following Generation X—was so dubbed by the magazine *Advertising Age*.

Q How does sugar rot your teeth?

A Remember the old commercial in which four out of five dentists recommended Trident chewing gum? You may not have realized it then, but Trident was the world's first sugarless gum—and we all know that dentists hate sugar because it causes tooth decay.

But what exactly is so corrosive about sugar? It starts with plaque. All of us, no matter how hard we brush, have plaque on our teeth. That's why it's so important to go to the dentist twice a year for the brutal scraping that removes the buildup of plaque. Plaque is kind of fascinating—in a disgusting way—because it is composed of millions of different kinds of bacteria that come together to form the translucent film on your teeth.

Your mouth isn't exactly the cleanest place, and bacteria love to feast on the same foods that you do—especially sugar. In fact, eating sugar is like dumping gasoline onto the inferno of bacteria that is already raging inside your mouth.

It turns out that bacteria process sugar much like people do. If you've ever gotten a jittery rush from eating a candy bar, you know that sugar can be converted into energy quite quickly. Bacteria react in the same manic way, though there's a corrosive twist. When bacteria (or any organism, for that matter) break down sugar into energy, the byproduct is several types of acid, including lactic acid. This process is known as glycolysis. Lactic acid, when built up over time, can start to eat away at the calcium phosphate in your tooth enamel; this is the beginning of a cavity.

So don't be deceived by sugar. There's nothing sweet about it.

Q How come the Three Musketeers didn't fight with muskets?

A Alexandre Dumas, a nineteenth-century French author, wrote hundreds of books, plays, articles, and essays. Much of this prodigious output was due to his "writing factory," in which assistants collaborated, with Dumas's input, to produce the work that bore his name. There's an old advertising adage that says, "A camel is a horse designed by committee"; it's just too bad that bit of wisdom wasn't around in Alex's day—it might have prevented him and his assistants from composing a novel about musketeers without putting any muskets in it.

The Three Musketeers is one of the most famous adventure novels in history. For those of you who lived in a cave during childhood, the historical novel follows the trials and travails of His Majesty's Guards Athos, Porthos, and Aramis, and their young protégé D'Artagnan, as they attempt to save the French crown from the secret machinations of Cardinal Richelieu and a mysterious woman named Milady.

Dumas based his tale on real people and events in French history; in fact, literary historians argue that Dumas paved the way for the historical novel of today. Musketeers—or *mousquetaires*—were sixteenth- and seventeenth-century European soldiers who were armed with the new technological weapon of the age, the musket. France had two elite units of musket-bearing soldiers: the *mousquetaires gris* and *mousquetaires noirs*. These soldiers were equally known for their fighting ability and their panache.

Unfortunately, the musket wasn't a practical weapon. The guns could measure longer than five feet and weigh more than twenty pounds. In fact, most musketeers had to carry a separate device just to keep the musket propped up while firing—hardly the kind of weaponry that lent itself to stylish hand-to-hand battles.

Not surprisingly, muskets fell out of favor with elite soldiers who needed mobility, but the "musketeers" name stuck. Athos, Porthos, and Aramis, as members of the king's elite guard, wouldn't have had much use for unwieldy guns that required several minutes to reload. Instead, they relied on their swords, charm, and delightfully plumed hats.

Though Dumas gestured toward historical accuracy in his works, he wasn't too concerned about it. In truth, Dumas's extravagant tastes and desire for the limelight made him far too worried about cranking out formulaic, plot-heavy tales to concern himself with little details like consistency, believability, theme, or character development. Which leads us to conclude that while literary historians may call Dumas one of the fathers of the historical novel, he seems more like the forefather of writing for another medium: television.

Q How long is a New York minute?

A New Yorkers have a reputation for being rude, provincial, haughty, and hurried—and for good reason. They won't hesitate to tell you that there are no bagels like New York bagels, no delis like New York delis, no theaters like Broadway theaters, no avenue like Fifth Avenue, and no team like the Yankees. New Yorkers even seem to believe that their units of time are superior to the pedestrian measurements the rest of us use. Think a minute lasts sixty seconds? Not in New York.

Sometimes a minute can seem like a pretty long time. Try holding your breath for a minute. Or holding a sack of cement. Or watching an episode of *Grey's Anatomy*. Or speaking with a New Yorker. And sometimes the word "minute" merely signifies a short, indefinite period of time—consider how we use the word colloquially, as in, "I'll be back in a minute" or "I was into that band for, like, a minute." The phrase "New York minute" carries a similar meaning.

Ironically, it doesn't appear as if New Yorkers coined the phrase. According to most etymologists, it probably originated in Texas. The disdain of Texans for New Yorkers (or just about any city slickers) might be thinly masked, but "New York minute" isn't really that much of an insult.

In popular usage, it merely means a short unit of time, possibly playing on the idea that life in New York City is hectic and a minute in the hurried atmosphere of the Big Apple passes more quickly than in the rest of the world. How fast? Well, according to *The* (Galveston, Tex.) *Daily News*, where the phrase first appeared in print in 1954, a New York minute lasts about thirty seconds.

But a New York minute might be even shorter than that. As Johnny Carson once put it, a New York minute is the amount of time that lapses between the light changing to green and the jerk behind you starting to honk.

Q How do vaccines work?

A If you've ever taken a small child to the doctor for a vaccination, you've probably had to explain that a little bit of hurt—a shot, a finger prick, a dose of sour-tasting medicine—can go a long way toward keeping us well. Then that pesky kid invariably asks, "Why?" You shrug and say, "I don't know. It just does, that's all."

Well, here's a better answer to give: superheroes. Your body has its very own superheroes called T cells and B cells. They're both part of your immune system and kick in whenever a virus shows up. Viruses are tiny microbes that can't live outside a body, so once they get inside you, they want to stay and pretty much take over the place. That's when T cells and B cells go to work and kick some butt.

First, "helper" T cells act as scouts, alerting the rest of your immune system to the presence of the invader and relaying the lowdown on its molecular composition. Then "killer" T cells swing into action, destroying any body cells that have been damaged by the virus. Meanwhile, B cells sweep your blood stream to seek out invaders. When they find a viral microbe, the B cells seize it by releasing special antibodies that lock onto the molecules of the virus, slowing it down and making it possible for large white blood cells called macrophages (the foot soldiers of the immune system) to come and eliminate it. Only one type of antibody will capture any given virus. Once the virus has been defeated, your immune system will remember which antibody it used and will be prepared should that particular unwelcome guest show up again.

What does all of this have to do with vaccines? When you are vaccinated, a doctor injects a tiny bit of a disease into your body. This may consist of a few very weak microbes or an artificial duplicate that researchers produce in a lab. Your body reacts as if the virus is the real thing—it's kind of like having an immune system fire drill. Your B cells manufacture the correct antibodies and add them to your arsenal of immune defenses. In short, you now have superpowers against some dangerous diseases. Pretty cool, huh?

Why don't vaccines work against every disease? Because not all illnesses are brought on by viruses. Some are caused by bacteria and cured by antibiotics. Some are the result of poor nutrition. Others have no known cure. The vaccinations we do have, however, make the world a much healthier place. They have helped many of us live long and prosper. And it doesn't get much more super than that.

Q How come nobody else calls it soccer?

A Millions of kids across the United States grow up playing a game that their parents hardly know, a game that virtually everyone else in the world calls football. It's soccer to us, of course, and although Americans might be ridiculed for calling it this, the corruption is actually British in origin.

Soccer—football, as the Brits and billions of others insist—has an ancient history. Evidence of games resembling soccer has been found in cultures that date to the third century BC. The Greeks had a version that they called *episkyro*. The Romans brought their version of the sport along when they colonized what is now England and Ireland. Over the next millennium, the game evolved into a freewheeling, roughneck competition—matches often involved kicking, shoving, and punching.

In England and Ireland, the sport was referred to as football; local and regional rules varied widely. Two different games—football and rugby—slowly emerged from this disorganized mess. The Football Association was formed in 1863 to standardize the rules of football and to separate it from rugby. The term "soccer" most likely is derived from the association's work.

During the late nineteenth century, the Brits developed the linguistic habit of shortening words and adding "-ers" or "-er." (We suffer this quirk to this day in expressions like "preggers." A red card to the Brits on this one.) One popular theory holds that given the trend, it was natural that those playing "Assoc." football were playing "assoccers" or "soccer." The term died out in England, but was revived in the United States in the early part of the twentieth century to separate the imported sport with the round white ball from the American sport with the oblong brown ball.

Soccer has long struggled to catch on as a major spectator sport in the United States. For most Americans, there just isn't enough scoring or action. In fact, many Yanks have their own word for soccer: boring.

Q How come some animals are equipped with horns?

A Ever locked horns with someone? Unless you have a very unusual skull, you were only butting heads meta-phorically. (We hope.) But male deer literally do lock horns in annual head-butting contests, which determine the buck that will win the affections of the fertile does. Each buck tries to force its opponent's head lower. On rare occasions, their antlers become so thoroughly interlocked that they cannot separate; they eventually starve to death together. It's a high price to pay for a little showing off.

Although antlers can be used to deter predators, zoologists believe that their main purpose is to impress the opposite sex. Among deer, an elaborate set of antlers is a way of saying, "I've got great genes!"

Technically, antlers and horns, both of which are composed of bone, are not quite the same thing. True horns—which are found on bovines, such as sheep, goats, and cattle—are coated with keratin, the same protein substance that forms human fingernails and animal hoofs. They appear on both males and females, though male horns are usually larger. Horns come in a variety of shapes—straight, curved, curled, twisted, or spiraled—but they are not branched like antlers. If broken, they cannot regenerate.

Horns on domestic animals are often blunted or filed down by their owners to prevent the animals from hurting themselves or others. Because most livestock breeding is accomplished by artificial insemination these days, head-butting competitions are a thing of the past on the ranch, and horns are an evolutionary adaptation that is no longer needed.

Antlers belong to beasts from the cervidae family, which includes deer, elk, caribou, and moose. Unlike horns, antlers are not covered by keratin, and they are shed every year in the winter; they regenerate in the spring. Only males have antlers, with the exception of caribou. Females of this species sport antlers, too (leading some "Santa-ologists" to suspect that Rudolph the Red-Nosed Reindeer may have actually been a girl).

Most antlers are sharp and multipronged—the better with which to fight. The spoon-shaped, or palmated, antlers of moose, however, do double duty as hearing aids. A particularly good set of antlers can boost a male moose's hearing nearly 20 percent by funneling sound toward the ear. Since moose tend to be solitary creatures, this can provide a distinct advantage in locating potential mates.

What about other "horned" animals? The narwhal whale has a long tusk that sometimes appears to be a horn, though it is actually formed from the same material as teeth. Horned lizards have bony projections on their heads and spine that they use for defense; they inflate themselves, forming a spiny balloon that protects them from predators.

Rhinoceros horns are composed entirely of keratin, with no bone at all. These horns are unique among mammals because they sit not atop the head, but on the forehead and above the nose. Full-grown rhinos have few predators, but they can use their horns to defend their young and, of course, to attract romance—proving once more that beauty is in the eye of the beholder.

Q How come golfers wear such ridiculous attire?

A In most of the major sports, athletes don't have much choice when it comes to what they wear. Basketball, football, baseball, and hockey teams all have uniforms. But other athletes aren't so lucky (and neither are their fans). Golfers, for example, are allowed to choose their own garb, leading to a parade of "uniforms" that look as if they were stitched together by a band of deranged clowns.

Why big-time golfers wear such hideous clothes is a source of bewilderment. Some apologists blame it on the Scots. Golf, after all, was supposedly invented by shepherds in Scotland back in the twelfth century, and it almost goes without saying that a sport born in a country where man-skirts are considered fashionable is doomed from the start. We'd like to point out that we are no longer in twelfth-century Scotland—let's move on, people.

But history may indeed play a role in golf's repeated fashion disasters. Kings and queens were reputed to have hit the links in the sixteenth and seventeenth centuries, and by the late nineteenth century, golf was a popular pastime amongst the nobility of England and Scotland. The nobility, however, wasn't exactly known for its athletic prowess. The other "sports" these noblemen participated in were activities like steeplechase (which has its own awful fashion), so many early golfers had no idea what types of clothes would be appropriate for an athletic endeavor. Early golfers simply took to the links wearing the fashionable attire of the day—attire that, unfortunately, included breeches and ruffled cravats (these were like neckties).

The tradition of wearing stuffy, silly attire continued into the twentieth century (as did the tradition of wealthy, paunchy white guys playing the sport), with awful sweaters and polyester pants replacing the ruffled cravats and knee-length knickers. Yet, remarkably, modern golfers take umbrage at the stereotype that duffers have no sense of fashion. According to one golf wag, the knock on golfers for being the world's worst-dressed athletes is unfair because nowadays almost everybody wears Dockers and polo shirts. (We'll pause while that gem sinks in.)

To be fair, the dreadful golf fashions of the 1970s and 1980s have given way to a more benign blandness that is at least less offensive, if not remotely what anybody would call "stylish." Of course, all fashion is less offensive than it was in the 1970s and 1980s, so perhaps golf fashion is proportionally no better.

"Golf," Mark Twain once complained, "is a good walk spoiled." We love Mark Twain, but we have to say that spoiling a good walk is the least of golf's transgressions.

Q How do carrier pigeons know where to go?

A No family vacation would be complete without at least one episode of Dad grimly staring straight ahead, gripping the steering wheel, and declaring that he is not lost as Mom insists on stopping for directions. Meanwhile, the kids are tired, night is falling, and nobody's eaten anything except a handful of Cheetos for the past six hours. But Dad is not lost. He will not stop.

It's well known that men believe they have some sort of innate directional ability—and why not? If a creature as dull and dim-witted as a carrier pigeon can find its way home without any maps or directions from gas-station attendants, a healthy human male should certainly be able to do the same.

Little does Dad know that the carrier pigeon has a secret weapon. It's called magnetite, and its recent discovery in the beaks of carrier pigeons may help solve the centuries-old mystery of just how carrier pigeons know their way home.

Since the fifth century BC, when they were used for communication between Syria and Persia, carrier pigeons have been prized for their ability to find their way home, sometimes over distances of more than five hundred miles. In World War I and World War II, Allied forces made heavy use of carrier pigeons, sending messages with them from base to base to avoid having radio signals intercepted or if the terrain prevented a clear signal. In fact, several carrier pigeons were honored with war medals.

For a long time, there was no solid evidence to explain how these birds were able to find their way anywhere, despite theories that ranged from an uncanny astronomical sense to a heightened olfactory ability to an exceptional sense of hearing. Recently, though, scientists made an important discovery: bits of magnetic crystal, called magnetite, embedded in the beaks of carrier pigeons. This has led some researchers to believe that carrier pigeons have magneto reception—the ability to detect changes in the earth's magnetic fields—which is a sort of built-in compass that guides these birds to their destinations.

Scientists verified the important role of magnetite through a study that examined the effects of magnetic fields on the birds' homing ability. When the scientists blocked the birds' magnetic ability by attaching small magnets to their beaks, the pigeons' ability to orient themselves plummeted by almost 50 percent. There was no report, however, on whether this handicap stopped male pigeons from plunging blindly forward. We'd guess not.

Q How many people live at the North Pole besides Santa and his elves?

A The population at the North Pole is as transient as the terrain itself, which is in a constant state of flux due to shifting and melting ice. Human life in this frigid region consists of researchers floating on makeshift stations and tourists who aren't the sit-on-a-beach-in-the-Bahamas type. There are no permanent residents at the North Pole—save, of course, for Santa Claus and his posse.

When you're talking about the North Pole, you're referring to four different locales: geographic, magnetic, geomagnetic, and the pole of inaccessibility. The geographic North Pole, known as true north or ninety degrees north, is where all longitudinal lines converge. It sits roughly four hundred fifty miles north of Greenland, in the center of the Arctic Ocean. The magnetic pole—the point marker for compasses—is located about one hundred miles south of the geographic pole, northwest of the Queen Elizabeth Islands, which are part of northern Canada. Its position moves about twenty-five miles annually. In fact, the magnetic pole has drifted hundreds of miles from its point of discovery in 1831. Then there's the North Geomagnetic Pole, the northern end of the axis of the magnetosphere, the geomagnetic field that surrounds the earth and extends into space. Last is the Northern Pole of Inaccessibility, the point in the Arctic Ocean that is most distant from any landmass.

If the North Pole were more like its counterpart on the other end of the earth, the South Pole, it would be a lot more accessible. Since the South Pole is located on a continent, Antarctica, permanent settlements can be established. In fact, research stations at the South Pole have been in place since 1956. These bases range in population size, but most average fifteen personnel in winter (April to November) and one hundred fifty in summer (December to March). Combined, the stations house a few thousand people in the summer. The U.S. McMurdo Station alone might exceed a thousand individuals at the peak time of year.

All of this helps explain why Santa chose to live at the North Pole rather than the South Pole. If you're S. Claus and you don't want to be found, there isn't a better place than the North Pole to set up shop, even if that shop is always in danger of floating away.

Q How come old men wear their pants so high?

A Age is the great equalizer. No matter how hot you are when you're young, no matter how cool and stylish you manage to look through adulthood and into middle age, Father Time always has the last laugh. Our Q&A medical staff refers to it as the "Old Coot" stage of life.

Among the afflictions that the male body must endure as it enters the "Old Coot" stage are two significant and merciless adjustments to the physique: (1) Fat gathers around the abdominal area while disappearing from other areas, and (2) muscle tone deteriorates. This translates to an expansion of the midsection and a simultane-ous reduction in the hips and buttocks. In layman's terms, we call this a huge gut and no butt. And it adds up to a cruel sartorial reality: Your body has lost its shape, so your pants won't stay up.

Your pants need a waist and a butt to hang from. Once you lose those features, the only thing left to work with is that giant spare tire that you call a belly. So you've got to hike those pants up over the bulge and tighten your belt for dear life.

Go ahead and laugh now, but beware: One day, as you stand in front of the mirror, distracted by the inexplicably long hairs that are growing from your nostrils, your mild alarm will turn to sheer terror as your fancy low-riding pants fall down around your ankles.

Q How do people swallow swords?

A Verrry carefully. There are ways to fake it—such as using a trick sword with a plastic blade that collapses into the hilt—but authentic sword swallowing is no optical illusion. The blade isn't as sharp as that of a normal sword, but that doesn't change the fact that the swallower is pushing a hard metal shaft deep into his or her body.

Ironically, one of the essential skills of sword swallowing is not swallowing. When you stand and face upward, your upper gastro-intestinal tract—the passageway that's made up of your throat, pharynx, esophagus, and stomach—is straight and flexible enough that a sword can pass through it. When you swallow, muscles contract and expand along the passageway in order to move food down to your stomach. Two sphincters along this tract—the upper esophageal sphincter between your pharynx and esophagus and the lower esophageal sphincter between your esophagus and stomach—are normally closed; they open involuntarily as food moves past. To keep the passageway clear, the swallower must learn deep relaxation techniques to resist the urge to swallow.

Sword swallowers also have to suppress their gag reflex, an automatic muscle contraction triggered when nerve endings in the back of the throat sense a foreign object. To deactivate the gag reflex, a sword swallower crams progressively larger objects into the back of the throat while trying not to gag. After hours of disgusting noises and periodic vomiting, the gag reflex is suitably numbed and the aspiring swallower can get down to business.

As the sword slides down the gastrointestinal tract all the way into the stomach, it straightens the various curves of the tract. Some swallowers coat their swords with a lubricant, such as olive oil, to help them along.

This mind-over-matter feat is one of the oldest stunts there is. Historians believe that the practice originated in India around 2000 BC, as a part of rituals designed to demonstrate powerful connections to the gods. The ancient Romans, Greeks, and Chinese picked up the practice, but generally viewed it as entertainment rather than religious observance. Sword swallowers at the 1893 World's Fair in Chicago sparked America's interest in the spectacle, and it soon became a staple of traveling sideshows.

Did we mention that you shouldn't try this trick at home? It goes without saying that sword swallowing is a dangerous and generally ill-advised endeavor. Even master swallowers sustain injuries—cram a sword, even a dull one, down your throat enough times, and you're likely to nick something important. If you must impress your friends, stick with more manageable sharp objects, such as Doritos.

Q How did Groundhog Day get started?

A It wasn't the brainchild of Punxsutawney Phil, the world's most famous weather-predicting groundhog. February 2, the day we observe as Groundhog Day, is important in the seasonal cycle. It falls halfway between the winter solstice—the shortest day of the year in the Northern Hemisphere—and the spring equinox, which is one of two days of equal sunlight and darkness.

This midpoint between winter and spring brings anticipation of a weather change from harsh cold to pleasant warmth. If we humans have an opportunity to believe that warm weather may come sooner rather than later, we'll take it. So weather predicting became tied to this day.

The ancient Celts marked this halfway point with a holiday called Imbolc. Early Christians, meanwhile, routinely scheduled holidays to compete with and replace pagan holidays. February 2 is forty days after December 25, so Imbolc became Candlemas Day, an observance of the day Mary and Joseph took Jesus to the temple to perform the redemption of the firstborn. It was celebrated as a sort of end to the Christmas season.

The weather-predicting aspect of Candlemas Day carried over from pagan traditions. Europeans would place a candle in their windows on the eve of Candlemas Day. If the sun was out the next morning, they believed it indicated that there would be six more weeks of winter.

The predicting tools varied across Europe; in some places, they involved animals, such as bears, badgers, and, in Germany, the hedgehog. But requirements were the same: If it was sunny and the animal cast a shadow, it meant a longer winter; if it was cloudy and there was no shadow, it meant a shorter winter. When the hedgehog-watching Germans came to hedgehog-free America, they became groundhog-watching Americans. The earliest reference to Groundhog Day in America can be found in an 1841 diary by James Morris, a Pennsylvania shop owner.

With such a proud legacy, groundhogs can be counted on to be correct most of the time, right? Think again. A Canadian study showed that groundhogs are correct in predicting the length of winter only about 37 percent of the time.

Q How come everyone claps so much during the State of the Union address?

Earlier tonight, it was George Bush's State of the Union address . . . He was interrupted forty times by applause and twice to look up a word in the dictionary.

—David Letterman

A The Constitution requires only that the President "shall from time to time give to Congress information of the

State of the Union and recommend to their consideration such measures as he shall judge necessary and expedient." There's nothing in there mandating massive applause, but it's a signature of the occasion just the same.

The State of the Union was meant to be like the British monarch's Speech from the Throne, given at the opening of Parliament each year. George Washington gave the first State of the Union speech in January 1790. Third president Thomas Jefferson thought the practice was too British and instead sent a written statement to be read by a clerk; this was the standard until Woodrow Wilson delivered the message to Congress in 1913. Calvin Coolidge's 1923 speech was the first to be broadcast on the radio; Harry Truman's in 1947 was the first to be shown on television; and George W. Bush's in 2002 was the first to be Webcast.

But what about the applause? The State of the Union address takes place in the U.S. Capitol Building, and begins when the Sergeant at Arms of the U.S. House of Representatives calls out, "Mister/Madam Speaker, the President of the United States!" The doors of the House Chamber are opened, and a standing ovation is expected. The members of Congress are not applauding the person—note that the Sergeant at Arms does not refer to the president by name—but rather the office of President.

Once the audience is settled, the Speaker of the House raps the gavel and again introduces the president—but not by name. Again, the applause is for the office. When the president begins to speak, he is interrupted by applause many times, some of which becomes partisan in nature. During George W. Bush's fifty-three-minute State of the Union speech in 2008, he was interrupted seventy-two times by applause, often only by Republicans. However, mentions of greenhouse gases and job retraining prompted Democrats to rise to their feet because these are Democratic party issues.

One member of Congress is notably absent from the State of the Union address because of the theoretical possibility that the country would be left without a leader if the Capitol Building were attacked and everyone were wiped out. This person, called the President pro Tempore of the Senate, watches the speech from some other location. No word on whether he or she applauds.

Q How do sniffer dogs know what to sniff?

A The same way musicians get to Carnegie Hall: practice, practice, and more practice.

From bloodhounds to bulldogs to Heinz 57s, almost any dog can be trained to follow scents. Doggie noses have twenty to forty times as many receptors as human snouts, which makes them more sensitive than the best man-made instruments. With the right training, dogs can learn to pick out faint traces of any scent—from the types of plastics used in DVDs to bugs or drugs. They may even be able to smell cancer and other diseases.

No matter what odor a dog is being trained to search for, the process is the same: Dogs are given various items to smell; when they sniff the target odor, they get a reward.

Want a dog to sniff out polycarbonate plastic so that it can find shipments of pirated DVDs at the airport? Several times a day for months, present the dog with a dozen or so choices. You might show it a bologna sandwich, a pen, a wallet, a stuffed animal, and finally a DVD—then give Fido a treat when it takes a whiff of the DVD.

After a few months, the dog associates the odor with praise and treats, and will go after it with passion. As a result of this kind of training, dogs learn how to search for bodies (either alive or dead), stolen money, drugs such as cocaine and marijuana, guns, explosives, land mines, termites, bedbugs, and even toxic mold. The latter takes the most intense training because there are different types of toxic mold that a good search dog must be able to zero in on.

Trained, certified canine sniffers are so sensitive that the U.S. courts recognize them as "scientific instruments." After becoming certified search dogs, canines must train for up to fifty hours a month to maintain their top form. Since the training involves doing what the dog loves to do anyway, training is more of a game than work—at least for the dog.

Toxic mold specialist Rick Koenig of Hermosa Beach, California, uses his sniffer pooch, Savannah, to detect mold in buildings. When he walked his dog into a large, multistory office building one day, the company's vice president was skeptical that a canine could do the job. The vice president laughed out loud when Savannah stopped and indicated that there was mold in a concrete filing unit on the ground floor of the building. The unit was waterproof, fireproof, leakproof—it was everything-proof. How could mold exist there? The unit was opened, and the gooey, moldy remains of a sandwich, hidden behind some files months before, vindicated Savannah. The VP became the dog's biggest champion.

Praise, treats, and a job well done—it's all in a day's work for a sniffer dog.

Q How is it that hair grows in all the wrong places as you age?

A Let's be honest: The older we get, the prettier we ain't. In addition to the sagging and the wrinkles, an ignominious side effect of aging is the dense thickets of hair that erupt from the ears, nose, and just about anywhere else you don't want them. While you have no choice but to accept the grim destiny of old age, you can at least know what cruel twist of anatomical fate produces this phenomenon.

Whether you are a man or woman, the culprit appears to be female hormones. And take notice of the word "appears." You should know up front that afflictions such as cancer and diabetes, not excessive nose hair, are what tend to get most of the medical attention and research funding. Consequently, the explanation that follows is mostly conjecture.

Both men and women produce female hormones such as estrogen. These hormones restrict the growth of body hair and counteract male-type hormones such as testosterone (which are also present in both men and women), which trigger the growth of body hair. When you're younger, the male and female hormones maintain the balance they should. As you get older, production of the female hormones slows down. In other words, the male–female hormonal balance gets out of whack, and you begin to look like a Yeti.

But it isn't all doom and gloom for old-timers: They get cheap movie tickets and can force people to sit through their long, rambling stories.

Q How does soap get us clean?

A You've been out working in the garden all day, getting down and dirty. Now it's time for a little wood ash and animal fat to get yourself clean. Jump in the shower, add some salt and vegetable oil to the mix, and you should be feeling fresh as a daisy.

Doesn't sound too promising, huh?

Well, it wouldn't be if you dumped all of the above over your head at once, but fortunately someone has already combined them into one easy-to-use package. It's called soap. Wood ash, fat, salt, and oil are the essential ingredients of soap. Every bar contains them (or their chemical equivalents), whether you got it for $0.99 at a drugstore or $9.99 at an exclusive boutique.

In soap-making, wood ash is boiled down in water to create a caustic solution otherwise known as lye. Under normal circumstances, lye is definitely not something you would want anywhere near your skin. But when you add fat, a mysterious transformation called saponification takes place. Basically, this means the lye and fat molecules join to create a single long molecule consisting of oxygen, carbon, hydrogen, and sodium. If you want to get all scientific, it's written like this: $CH_3\text{-}(CH_2)n\text{-}CONa$.

Now this molecule can perform a pretty nifty trick. The fatty carbon-hydrogen end you see on the far left gloms onto a tiny particle of grease or dirt on your skin. The sodium at the opposite end attaches itself to a water molecule, and whoosh—the grime slides off. In other words, a soap molecule is like a tiny chain with a hook for dirt at one end and water at the other.

Who were the first people to figure this out? Archaeologists have discovered evidence of soap making in the Near East going back to around 2800 BC. One possible theory is that the ashes of wood fires would become saturated with the fat of roasting animals. If it happened to rain before the ashes cooled, the ashes would start bubbling up in an interesting way. Eventually women discovered this strange bubbly stuff was good for scrubbing pots, garments, and the occasional squalling kid, too. Soap was born.

If you're worried about too many trees being sacrificed for cleanliness, rest assured that soap today is made largely from caustic soda produced artificially in a laboratory. And if you're a vegetarian, there are plenty of animal-free soaps to choose from. The idea behind their manufacture still remains the same, however. So grab a bar, thank your ancestors for this humble invention, and get yourself squeaky clean!

Q How can it rain cats and dogs?

A It can't. Many of us are familiar with strange-but-true stories that describe fish, frogs, or bugs raining from the sky. Indeed, waterspouts and odd, windy weather patterns can suck up small animals, carry them a few miles, and drop them from the sky. But nowhere on record are confirmed reports of it raining felines and canines.

It's a figure of speech, and its origins are unknown. However, that hasn't prevented etymologists from speculating. One unlikely theory claims that in days of yore, dogs and cats that were sleeping in the straw of thatched roofs would sometimes slip off the roof and fall to the ground during a rainstorm.

Almost as unlikely is the belief that the phrase was cobbled together from superstitions and mythology. Some cultures have associated cats with rain, and the Norse god Odin often was portrayed as being surrounded by dogs and wolves, which were associated with wind. (Anybody who's had an aging dog around the house can vouch for it being an occasional source of ill wind, but that's hardly the stuff of legend.) The components seem right with this one, but it's hard to imagine someone stitching everything together to coin a catchy phrase.

A couple of simpler theories seem more plausible. Some folks think that "cats and dogs" stems from the Greek word *catadupe* or the archaic French *catadoupe*, both meaning "waterfall." Others point to the Latin *cata doxas* ("contrary to experience").

The most believable explanation, however, is the least pleasant. The earliest uses of the term occur in English literature of the seventeenth and eighteenth centuries. Around that time in London, dead animals, including cats and dogs, were thrown out with the trash. Rains would sweep up the carcasses and wash them through the streets. Jonathan Swift used the phrase "rain cats and dogs" in his book *A Complete Collection of Polite and Ingenious*

Conversation in 1738. Twenty-eight years earlier, Swift had published a poem, "A Description of a City Shower," that included the lines: "Drown'd Puppies, stinking Sprats, all drench'd in Mud/ Dead Cats and Turnip-Tops come tumbling down the Flood."

Hardly a love sonnet, but perhaps it answers our question.

Q How do corked bats help cheating baseball players hit the ball farther?

A In this age of performance-enhancing drugs, it's almost refreshing when a hitter gets caught cheating the old-fashioned way. Corked bats somehow recall a more innocent time.

There are different ways to cork a wooden baseball bat, but the basic procedure goes like this: Drill a hole into the top of the bat, about an inch in diameter and twelve inches deep; fill the hole with cork—in rolled sheets or ground up—and close the top with a wooden plug that matches the bat; finally, stain and finish the top of the bat so that the plug blends in.

The supposed benefits of a corked bat involve weight and bat speed. Cork is lighter than wood, which enables a player to generate more speed when swinging the bat. The quicker the swing, the greater the force upon contact with the ball—and the farther that ball flies. The lighter weight allows a batter more time to evaluate a pitch, since he can make up the difference with his quicker swing; this extra time amounts to only a fraction of a second, but it can be the difference between a hit and an out at the major league level.

Following the logic we've set forth, replacing the wood in the bat with nothing at all would make for an even lighter bat and, thus, provide more of an advantage. The problem here is that an empty core would increase the likelihood that the bat would break; at the very least, it would cause a suspicious, hollow sound upon contact with the ball. The cork fills in the hollow area, and does so in a lightweight way.

Not everyone believes that a corked bat provides an advantage; some tests have indicated that the decreased bat density actually diminishes the force applied to the ball. But Dr. Robert Watts, a mechanical engineer at Tulane University who studies sports science, sees things differently. He concluded that corking a bat increases the speed of the swing by about 2.5 percent; consequently, the ball might travel an extra fifteen to twenty feet, a distance that would add numerous home runs to a player's total over the course of his career.

In any case, we haven't heard much lately about corked bats. That's because the headlines have been dominated by players who have used steroids to cork themselves.

Q How does a flak jacket stop a bullet?

 A "Flak" is an abbreviation of *Fliegerabwehrkanone*, a German word that looks rather silly (as many German words do). There's nothing silly, however, about its meaning: anti-aircraft cannon.

Serious development of flak jackets began during World War II, when Air Force gunners wore nylon vests with steel plates sewn into them as protection against shrapnel. After the war, manufacturers discovered that they could remove the steel plates and instead make the vests out of multiple layers of dense, heavily woven nylon.

Without the steel plates, the vests became a viable option for ground troops to wear during combat. Anywhere from sixteen to twenty-four layers of this nylon fabric were stitched together into a thick quilt. In the 1960s, DuPont developed Kevlar, a lightweight fiber that is five times stronger than a piece of steel of the same weight. Kevlar was added to flak jackets in 1975.

It seems inconceivable that any cloth could withstand the force of a bullet. The key, however, is in the construction of the fabric. In a flak jacket, the fibers are interlaced to form a super strong net. The fibers are twisted as they are woven, which adds to their density. Modern flak jackets also incorporate a coating of resin on the fibers and layers of plastic film between the layers of fabric. The result is a series of nets that are designed to bend but not break.

A bullet that hits the outer layers of the vest's material is flattened into a mushroomlike shape. The remaining layers of the vest can then dissipate the misshapen bullet's energy and prevent it from penetrating. The impact of the offending bullet usually leaves a bruise or blunt trauma to internal organs, which is a minor injury compared to the type of devastation a bullet is meant to inflict.

While no body armor is 100 percent impenetrable, flak jackets offer different levels of protection depending on the construction and materials involved. At the higher levels of protection, plates of lightweight steel or special ceramic are still used. But all flak jackets incorporate this netlike fabric as a first line of defense. *Fliegerabwehrkanone*, indeed.

Q How do we know that no two snowflakes are alike?

A Well, do you know the Snowflake Man? In 1885, Wilson Bentley became the first person to photograph a single snow crystal. By cleverly adapting a microscope to a bellows camera, the nineteen-year-old perfected a process that allowed him to catch snowflakes on a black-painted wooden tray and then capture their images before they melted away.

A self-educated farmer from the rural town of Jericho, Vermont, Bentley would go on to attract worldwide attention for his pioneering work in the field of photomicrography. In 1920, the American Meteorological Society elected him as a fellow and later awarded him its very first research grant, a whopping twenty-five dollars.

Over forty-seven years, Bentley captured 5,381 pictographs of individual snowflakes. Near the end of his life, the Snowflake Man said that he had never seen two snowflakes that were alike: "Under the microscope, I found that snowflakes were miracles of beauty. Every crystal was a masterpiece of design and no one design was ever repeated."

Since Bentley's original observation, physicists, snowologists, crystallographers, and meteorologists have continued to photograph and study the different patterns of ice-crystal growth and snowflake formation (with more technologically advanced equipment, of course). But guess what? Bentley's snow story sticks.

Even today, scientists agree: It is extremely unlikely that two snowflakes can be exactly alike. It's so unlikely, in fact, that Kenneth G. Libbrecht, a professor of physics at Caltech, says, "Even if you looked at every one ever made, you would not find any exact duplicates."

How so? Says Libbrecht, "The number of possible ways of making a complex snowflake is staggeringly large." A snowflake may start out as a speck of dust, but as it falls through the clouds, it gathers up more than 180 billion water molecules. These water molecules freeze, evaporate, and arrange themselves into endlessly inventive patterns under the influence of endless environmental conditions.

And that's just it—snow crystals are so sensitive to the tiniest fluctuations in temperature and atmosphere that they're constantly changing in shape and structure as they gently fall to the ground. Molecule for molecule, it's virtually impossible for two snow crystals to have the exact same pattern of development and design.

"It is probably safe to say that the possible number of snow crystal shapes exceeds the estimated number of atoms in the known universe," says Jon Nelson, a cloud physicist who has studied snowflakes for fifteen years. Still, we can't be 100 percent sure that no two snowflakes are exactly alike—we're just going to have to take science's word for it. Each winter, trillions upon trillions of snow crystals drop from the sky. Are you going to check them all out?

Q How come so many people are right-handed?

A Lefties have had it rough for thousands of years. Mocked, persecuted, prosecuted, and executed, left-handers have suffered ignominies that are evident in the word itself. *Sinistre*— the root of the English word sinister—means "left" in Latin, while *gauche*, absorbed into English as meaning "graceless and awkward," is the French term. It's no surprise that lefties are somewhat defensive about their handedness, forming associations and fellowships, and marching under a banner proudly proclaiming that "Lefties Are All Right."

Depending on whom you believe, about 10 to 25 percent of the population is left-handed. The reason for this is almost as much of a mystery as how handedness works in the first place. One dominant theory holds that left-handers are such a minority because of historical pressures. The left gained evil connotations with the advent of Christianity. For example, Satan baptized his followers with his left hand. And in Jesus's parable of the sheep and the goats, the goats were placed on J. C.'s left, symbolizing all who were to burn forever in hell.

It's not difficult to imagine, considering the power of Christianity during the last two millennia, that this fear of the left would spread throughout much of Western civilization. (Indeed, until well into the twentieth century, parochial school students could expect to receive a rap on the knuckles if they tried to write with their left hands.) This theory holds that the historical ostracizing of left-handers made them an unwanted group and far less likely to pass on their genetic predilection for evil. Still, left-handers had some natural advantages. Using the left hand gave them an advantage in combat, for example, which explains why left-handedness wasn't wiped out completely.

This theory earns points when one considers the results of, oddly, a survey about odor perception conducted in 1986. The survey was done by Charles J. Wysocki of the Monell Chemical Senses Center and Avery N. Gilbert of Givaudan-Roure Corp., and serendipitously revealed that the percentage of left-handers in the general population rose significantly during the twentieth century, as acceptance of southpaws increased in the popular mind-set. Furthermore, scientists studying handedness recently claimed to have found a gene that is associated with left-handedness, further supporting the idea that in the evolutionary game of natural selection, the outcast left-handed genes would have a slimmer chance of being passed along.

Despite the recent acceptance of left-handers by the rest of the world, it's clear that society is still designed for right-handers, as any left-handed college student struggling to write on one of those kidney-shaped lecture-hall desks made for righties can tell you. Still, the list of left-handed individuals who have achieved some level of greatness is impressive indeed. Alexander the Great, Napoleon, Einstein, Newton, Picasso, Leonardo da Vinci, Michelangelo, and Jimi Hendrix were all left-handed.

Plenty of famous politicians and statesmen exhibited sinistrality as well: Ramses II, Benjamin Franklin, a large percentage of the

British royal family, and numerous U.S. presidents (including the Reagan-Bush-Clinton trifecta from 1980 to 2000). Of course, many folks would claim that politicians are neither right-handed nor left-handed, but rather under-handed.

Q How come cats' eyes are so shiny?

A Ever see a cat's eyes shining at night? Pretty weird, right? How do cats do that? Do they use their eyes like we use headlights on a car—to find their way in the dark? To a certain degree, they do.

Cats have a special layer of cells in their eyes known as the *tapetum lucidum* (Latin for "shining carpet"). The tapetum is located behind the retina and acts as a mirror, catching and reflecting light. A cat's retina is composed of rods and cones, just like a human retina.

Cones are responsible for daylight vision and the ability to see colors; rods are used in night vision and for detecting sudden movements. As you may guess, night hunters, including cats, have eyes with a high ratio of rods to cones—twenty-five to one. (Human eyes have only four rods to every cone, which is why we have poor night vision.)

The tapetum lucidum is essentially a backup system for the rods in the cat's retina. The tightly clustered rods catch most of the available light at night, but some light inevitably slips by the rods. When this happens in humans, the light is simply absorbed by the back of the retina and lost—we can't use it to see. But in cats' eyes, this lost light hits the tapetum and is reflected back through the retina via the rods, giving these sensitive cells a second chance to use the light to enhance the cat's vision. This reflective process is what creates those spooky headlight eyes that have inspired so many Halloween cards.

In addition to the tapetum, the cat's elliptically shaped pupils give it an advantage at night. Cats' pupils can dilate very rapidly to fill almost the entire iris, letting in even more light. Some scientists think that the elliptical shape of the pupil enables the eye to utilize a wider-than-normal range of light waves, further enhancing vision. But this is only a theory—it's not a proven fact.

Other animals—including dogs, deer, fruit bats, dolphins, and some species of fish—have the tapetum lucidum, too, though their effects are not as pronounced as in cats. Research on the tapetum lucidum has been useful to the field of thin film optics, and has been applied to the development of mirrors and reflective lights to aid human night vision.

We will probably never be able to equal the cat's ability to see in the dark, however. Feline eyes are a unique and beautiful evolutionary adaptation. And a bit of Halloween, 365 nights a year.

Q How sweet are sweetbreads?

A tip for those who rarely eat at trendy restaurants: If you see sweetbreads on the menu, don't start salivating at the thought of a warm muffin with butter dripping down the sides. Instead, picture the thymus gland or pancreas of a young sheep, cow, or pig. Then exhale deeply and start focusing on taking a swig or two from your glass of wine.

Sweetbreads are a delicacy enjoyed throughout the world by people with adventurous palettes, but the burger-and-fries types might not understand such culinary wanderlust. In fact, they might want to ask the question: What in the name of the Golden Arches is a thymus gland? The answer isn't pretty. A thymus gland contains two lobes—one in the throat and the other near the heart. The lobe near the heart—particularly from milk-fed young calves—is considered the best to eat because of its smooth texture and mild taste; as a result, it will cost you more at that trendy restaurant. Pancreas sweetbreads, or stomach sweetbreads, are much less common than their thymus counterparts.

Sweetbreads and other edible internal organs are often grouped together using the term "offal" (which, for those still ready to vomit, isn't a word for "awful" in some foreign language). It means the "off-fall," or the off-cuts, of a carcass.

Since sweetbreads aren't sweet and aren't bread, how did they get their name? This is something of a mystery. The *historie of man*, published in 1578, sheds a splash of light on the matter: "A certaine Glandulous part, called Thimus, which in Calues . . . is most pleasaunt to be eaten. I suppose we call it the sweete bread." Translation: They tasted good.

Back in those roughhewn days—before butcher shops and grocery stores—sweetbreads weren't considered a delicacy. Families butchered their own livestock and often ate every part, including the thymus gland and pancreas. Today, sweetbreads are prepared in many ways: You can poach, roast, sear, braise, or sauté 'em, and often season them with salt, pepper, onions, garlic, or thyme.

If you want to prepare sweetbreads, we have two pieces of advice. First, sweetbreads are extremely perishable, so be sure to cook them within twenty-four hours of your purchase. Second, they're probably not the ideal dish to serve on a first date.

Q How do you become a saint?

A Everyone who has worked in an office environment has encountered that guy who thinks he should be a saint. You know, the only person who ever fills the copy machine with paper? The benevolent soul—the only one, to hear him tell it— who respects his coworkers enough to clean up after himself in the break room? Yeah, that guy. He should be a saint, right?

With apologies to Bob from Human Resources, becoming a saint is quite a bit more complicated than being punctual for staff meetings. Though most religions throughout history have honored particularly holy members in different ways, most people think of sainthood—at least in Western culture—in terms of Roman Catholicism. In the Catholic Church, the process of becoming a saint is known as canonization.

Though sainthood is the ultimate honor in the Catholic Church, good Christians who are destined to become saints won't know it during their lifetime—the canonization process starts after the candidate has died. In fact, there usually is a five-year waiting period after death before the Catholic Church will consider a candidate for sainthood. Once the waiting period is finished, local church officials will study the life and writings of the proposed saint to make sure that he or she lived a truly Christian life. If the person passes muster, the pope labels him or her "venerable."

The next step in canonization involves attributing a miracle—such as spontaneous healings at the candidate's grave or spontaneous appearances of holy images—to the now-venerable candidate. (Sorry, Bob, but filing your TPS report by deadline doesn't count.) Once the church determines that the miracle in question can be attributed to the candidate, that person is "beatified."

However, beatification still isn't enough to become a saint. Because anyone can get lucky and cure a paraplegic once—look, even a blind squirrel can stumble upon one nut—the church requires a second miracle to ensure that the first wasn't a fluke. Only after this second miracle is confirmed is the candidate officially made a saint.

There is a quicker way to sainthood—martyrdom. So if Bob from HR really wants to become a saint, there are probably plenty of volunteers who would help him along that path.

 How does the belly button gather so much lint?

 It's an affliction that embarrasses most people. Some call it "dirty" and "gross"; others simply find it mysterious.

When it is discussed, it's usually late at night, behind closed doors. Yes, we're referring to belly button lint. But if there's one thing we've learned in our weekly belly button lint support group, it's that this accumulation of fuzz is natural. Still, each evening as we shamefully dislodge another tuft of blue-gray lint, we wonder just where it comes from.

Fortunately for humanity, not one but two scientists have taken on the Herculean task of identifying the source and nature of belly button lint. In 2001, Australian researcher Dr. Karl Kruszelnicki embarked upon a massive survey of nearly five thousand people in order to identify the risk factors for belly button lint (BBL). What did he learn? The typical BBL sufferer is male, middle-aged, slightly paunchy, and has a hairy stomach and an "innie" navel. Kruszelnicki suggested that BBL is merely minute fibers that are shed by the clothes we wear every day. These fibers are channeled by abdominal hair into the belly button, where they collect until they are extracted. Dr. K opines that the reason most BBL is a blue-gray color is that blue jeans rub the most against the body.

Dr. Kruszelnicki's research was a landmark study in BBL, but it wasn't quite detailed enough for some people. Enter Austrian chemist Dr. Georg Steinhauser, who decided that it was necessary to spend three years of his life chemically analyzing more than five hundred samples of BBL, mostly of his own making. Along the way, Steinhauser discovered that BBL isn't merely fibers from clothes, as Kruszelnicki had believed, but also includes bits of dead skin and fat.

Steinhauser went even further, establishing a list of practices to discourage the development of BBL. Shaving the abdomen seems to be the most foolproof method, though this strategy is, of course, temporary. Wearing older clothes may also help, because they have fewer loose fibers than new duds. Additionally, a belly button ring appears to have some effect in preventing BBL.

But it's another Australian man (what is it with Aussies and belly button lint?) who has taken BBL research to a whole new level. Graham Barker has been collecting his own BBL—which he calls "navel fluff"—in jars since 1984, earning himself a spot in *Guinness World Records*. Thanks to Barker's courage, it is now safe for those afflicted with BBL to come out of the closet and show their lint-filled belly buttons to the world.

Q How many Germans were actually Nazis?

A The Nazis, or National Socialist German Workers' Party, ruled Germany with an iron fist from 1933 to 1945, but they never actually achieved official majority support from the German people, either in the form of votes or party membership.

Adolf Hitler became the Nazi Party chairman in 1921, but the German government banned the party in 1923 after a failed Nazi coup attempt. Hitler reconstituted the party in 1925 and, over the course of five years, built it from a peripheral splinter group into one of the leading conservative political parties in Germany. However, it still didn't have enough support to win a majority of votes in any election. In April 1932, Hitler garnered a mere 36.8 percent of the vote in his bid to become the leader of Germany, losing out to the incumbent, Paul von Hindenburg. That same year in July, however, the Nazis received 37.8 percent of the vote in parliamentary elections, the most among Germany's parties.

The second-biggest party, the Social Democratic Party, was threatened by the Nazi Party's rise, but it was more concerned about the advances made by Germany's Communist Party. To build a coalition between the Nazis and Social Democrats, Hindenburg appointed Hitler as the new chancellor on January 30, 1933. At that point, there were about 1.4 million card-carrying Nazi Party members, less than 3 percent of the German population.

The Social Democrats hoped to control Hitler more effectively by giving him nominal power. But as chancellor, Hitler got the foothold he needed to turn Germany into a totalitarian dictatorship. Hindenburg called for new parliamentary elections in March 1933, and the Nazis turned up their intimidation tactics to sway voters away from the opposition. But even after fighting dirty, the Nazis won only 43.9 percent of the vote. The following July, Hitler declared the Nazi Party the sole political party of Germany, effectively ending democratic rule.

Even under totalitarian oppression, most Germans never joined the Nazi Party. Hitler made membership mandatory for only higher-level civil servants and bureaucrats. In fact, from May 1933 to May 1939, party membership was, for the most part, closed—Hitler wanted the Nazis to include a select elite rather than the entire German population. According to the Nazi Party's official *Zentralkartei* (master file), there were 7.2 million Nazi Party members between its reconstitution in 1925 and its dissolution in May 1945, the vast majority of whom joined after Hitler came to power. Based on these numbers, only around 10 percent of Germany's citizens were card-carrying Nazis.

If you define Nazis more broadly, as people who believed in the party's cause, it's impossible to determine the actual number. After Germany's crushing defeat in World War II, people weren't exactly clamoring to confess their past Nazi loyalties.

Q How cool are cucumbers?

A In his poem "A New Song of New Similes," eighteenth-century English author John Gay wrote, "I'd be...cool as a cucumber could see the rest of womankind." Not at all unwittingly, Gay coined a phrase that has become part of our collective consciousness. But are cucumbers really all that cool?

Let's turn back the clock a few hundred years. Imagine you're in India, the supposed birthplace of the cucumber. It's about one hundred degrees in the shade. You've just polished off a dish of delectable but fiery hot vindaloo chicken, and now it feels like steam is shooting out of your ears and nostrils, like you're a character in a Warner Brothers cartoon. Instinctively, you reach for a glass of ice water. But wait! In your dizzy, sweaty haste, you've forgotten that refrigeration—and Warner Brothers cartoons, for that matter—won't be invented for centuries.

There is no ice water! How do you extinguish the fire that rages in your mouth? That's right: You reach for a few slices of cool cucumber, and they really hit the spot.

While there's no reason to believe that its physical temperature is lower than that of any other vegetable, the cucumber's mild flavor and watery flesh give it a refreshing quality that has made it a favorite warm-weather ingredient in cooling salads, relishes, and yogurt sauces for generations. It should come as no surprise that the cucumber hails from the same family of plants (Cucurbiticeae) as the watermelon.

But there is evidence to suggest that cucumbers can keep you "cool" in other ways. The cucumber's skin is a source of fiber, and several studies have shown that a high-fiber diet may help to lower your blood pressure, a benefit for those who share some of the personality traits of certain steam-shooting cartoon characters. And when applied directly to the skin, the ascorbic acid (vitamin C) and caffeic acid found in the cucumber can help soothe and seemingly cool irritations and reduce swelling.

You may have heard of another, nondietary use for cucumbers: Rock stars have been known to stuff them into their pants to enhance a certain physical feature. The "prop" couldn't be sillier, but they think it makes them look cool.

Q How come metal sparks in a microwave?

A Microwave ovens work by permeating your food with microwave radiation. That sounds a little scary, but don't worry: We're not talking about the kind of radiation that gave us the giant lizard that stomped Tokyo. Instead, this radiation excites the water molecules that make up a large portion of every kind of food we eat. The vibrating water molecules start to get hot, which in turn heats the food.

Simple so far, right? It gets a little trickier. Metal responds quite differently to the electromagnetic field that a microwave oven creates. Unlike water, which can absorb the microwave energy, metal *reflects* the radiation. And the energy of the electromagnetic field can also cause a charge to build up in metal—especially if the metal is thin and pointy, like the tines of a fork, the handle of a Chinese take-out box, or the decorative rim on your Young Elvis commemorative plate.

When enough of a charge builds up, all of that energy in the metal can leap joyfully through the air. We see this leap as a spark—like a small-scale bolt of lightning. These arcs of electricity are most likely to emanate from sharp edges, like the tines of a fork or the ridges of crumpled aluminum foil. A solid object with no sharp edges should be okay, because any electrical charge that develops is more likely to spread itself around evenly.

But even then, there's a danger—the metal could reflect the microwave radiation back at the magnetron tube that creates the electromagnetic field. This could damage the magnetron tube, and then you'd be stuck with a useless microwave.

So here's an equation for you: metal + microwave = really bad idea. Stick to food.

Q How come Esperanto never caught on?

 Esperanto has fallen short of the hopes of its creator, L. L. Zamenhof, but it has by no means been a flop. When the

Russian-born Zamenhof unveiled Esperanto in 1887, he envisioned it as a flexible world language that would become the shared tongue of governments everywhere and would promote peace and understanding. Although Esperanto never became that pervasive, for decades it has been the most used "model" or "constructed" language in the world, with estimates of current users ranging as high as two million. That's more than the speakers of many natural languages, such as those spoken by Native Americans, aboriginal populations on other continents, and European minority peoples.

According to estimates, there are a few hundred to about a thousand native speakers of Esperanto—folks whose parents taught them the language as a baby. Among these is gazillionaire Hungarian financier, activist, and philanthropist George Soros. Although Soros can stay in—or buy, for crying out loud—any hotel in the world, he can also use his Esperanto to secure lodgings with any other Esperantist in roughly ninety countries, one of the language's endearing features.

Thousands of books have been published in Esperanto, including original and translated works; there are Esperanto television and radio broadcasts, magazines, and an annual world congress that attracts an average of two thousand attendees. Its proponents say it is up to twenty times easier to learn than other languages.

So why didn't Esperanto succeed on Zamenhof's terms? There are several reasons:

• Given the disparity of languages in the world, it is impossible to construct a vocabulary and grammar that doesn't pose serious challenges to someone.

- The language's sounds are too similar to Zamenhof's native Belarussian, making pronunciation hard for many. Culturally speaking, it is European in its vocabulary and semantics.

- The vocabulary is unnecessarily large, due to the constant additions of new word roots rather than new words being based on old ones.

- Esperanto and its speakers have been the subject of persecution. It was outlawed in communist Russia until 1956, and Esperanto speakers have been killed under totalitarian regimes. Hitler claimed it could become the language of an international Jewish conspiracy, which was a testament to both Esperanto's success and Hitler's insanity.

But the biggest strike against the language is that it sprung from no shared natural culture. To grow large, a language needs a considerable group of people speaking together daily and developing close associations among their shared experiences and shared words.

Languages are an outgrowth of human behavior and history, not the result of well-intentioned intellectual efforts. Put it this way: Any language whose biggest gabfest is an annual world congress isn't going to take over the world.

Still, Esperanto was and is a success. Consider this: Around the time Zamenhof was inventing Esperanto, a German priest, who was acting on something God told him in a dream, invented Volapük. The language got off to a fast start, but today it's estimated that only a few dozen people speak Volapük. Now that's a lonely world congress.

Q How does a gas pump nozzle know when your tank is full?

A When you've maxed out your credit card, of course. Actually, the system is entirely mechanical and completely impervious to financial matters.

The mechanism at work is a little complicated, but the basic idea is fairly straightforward. As gas flows, it generates suction inside the nozzle, thanks to something called the Venturi effect. A fuel nozzle uses this suction to gauge whether there's any air at the end of the nozzle spout.

In the nozzle, the gas passes through a Venturi ring, a narrow passageway with tiny openings that lead to an air chamber. This air chamber is connected to a long tube that leads to a hole near the end of the nozzle spout, just under the larger hole where the gas comes out. Essentially, this tube is a straw for sucking air from the tank. As the fuel flows through the ring, the suction from the Venturi effect reduces air pressure in the chamber. Air rushes from the tank through the tube to equalize the pressure, in the same way soda rushes through a straw to equalize a drop in pressure in your mouth.

As long as there is room in the tank, the system will keep sucking in air and the pressure in the chamber will stay close to normal atmospheric levels. But when the gasoline reaches the tip of the nozzle, no more air can get through the little hole and the pressure in the chamber drops. This increased suction pulls on a diaphragm connected to the nozzle's shut-off valve, which closes to stop the flow of gasoline.

If you try to keep pumping to "top off" the tank, you might actually be pumping money out of your wallet. According to the Environmental Protection Agency, when there's no room in the tank, extra gas can flow up through vapor recovery lines in the pump that are designed to prevent gas vapor from polluting the atmosphere. As a result, you may be paying to pump gas back into the station's tanks. Haven't you given them enough already?

Q How do fireworks form different shapes?

A Fireworks have been delighting people (and on the negative side, blowing off fingers) for more than seven hundred years, and the design hasn't changed much in that time. Getting those fireworks to form complex shapes is a tricky challenge, but the basic idea is still fairly old-school.

To understand what's involved, it helps to know some fireworks basics. A fireworks shell is a heavy paper container that holds three sections of explosives. The first section is the "lift charge," a packet of black powder (a mixture of potassium nitrate, sulphur, and charcoal) at the bottom of the shell. To prepare the shell for launch, a pyrotechnician places the shell in a mortar (a tube that has the same diameter as the shell), with the lift charge facing downward. A quick-burning fuse runs from the lift charge to the top of the mortar. To fire the shell, an electric trigger lights the quick fuse. It burns down to ignite the black powder at the bottom of the shell, and the resulting explosion propels the shell out of the mortar and high into the air.

The second explosive section is the "bursting charge," a packet of black powder in the middle of the shell. When the electric trigger lights the quick-burning fuse, it also lights a time-delay fuse that runs to the bursting charge. As the shell is hurtling through the air, the time-delay fuse is burning down. Around the time the shell reaches its highest point, the fuse burns down to the bursting charge, and the black powder explodes.

Expanding black powder isn't exactly breathtaking to watch. The vibrant colors you see come from the third section of explosives, known as the "stars." Stars are simply solid clumps of explosive metals that emit colored light when they burn. For example, burning copper salts emit blue light and burning barium nitrate emits green light. The expanding black powder ignites the stars and propels them outward, creating colored streaks in the sky.

The shape of the explosion depends on how the manufacturer positions the stars in the shell. To make a simple ring, it places the stars in a ring around the bursting charge; to make a heart, it positions the stars in a heart shape. Manufacturers can make more complex fireworks patterns, such as a smiley face, by combining multiple compartments with separate bursting charges and stars in a single shell. As the fuse burns, these different "breaks" go off in sequence. In a smiley face shell, the first break that explodes makes a ring, the second creates two dots for the eyes, and the third forms a crescent shape for the mouth.

It's hard to produce designs that are much more complex than that, since only a few breaks can be set off in quick succession. So if you're hoping to see a fireworks tribute to origami, you're out of luck.

Q How did the biathlon become an Olympic event?

A It's one thing to ski through the frozen countryside; it's quite another to interrupt that heart-pounding exertion and muster up the calm and concentration needed to hit a target that's a few centimeters wide with a .22-caliber bolt-action rifle.

Yes, the biathlon is an odd sport. Cross-country skiing combined with rifle marksmanship? Why not curling and long jump? Figure skating and weight lifting? In actuality, however, the two skills that make up the biathlon have a history of going hand in hand, so combining them as an Olympic event makes perfect sense.

It's no surprise that the inspiration for the biathlon came from the frigid expanses of northern Europe, where there's not much to do in the winter besides ski around and drink aquavit. Cross-country skiing provides a quick and efficient way to travel over the snowy ground, so northern cultures mastered the technique early—and it was especially useful when it came time to hunt for winter food. People on skis were killing deer with bows and arrows long before such an activity was considered a sport.

But skiing and shooting (with guns, eventually) evolved from an act of survival into a competition. The earliest biathlon competitions were held in 1767 as informal contests between Swedish and Norwegian border patrols. The sport spread through Scandinavia in the nineteenth century as sharpshooting skiers formed biathlon clubs. In 1924, it was included as a demonstration sport in the Winter Olympics in Chamonix, France, although it was called military patrol.

In 1948, the Union Internationale de Pentathlon Moderne et Biathlon—the first international governing body for the sport—was formed. The official rules for what would come to be the modern biathlon were determined over the next several years.

During the 1960 Olympics at Squaw Valley Ski Resort in California, a biathlon was contested as an official Olympic event for the first time. The sport has evolved over the decades—it now features smaller-caliber rifles, different distances, various types of relays, and the participation of women. (A women's biathlon was first staged as an Olympic event in 1992 in Albertville, France.)

Today, biathlon clubs and organizations are active all over the world, and there are versions of the sport for summer in which running replaces skiing. Still, the biathlon's popularity remains strongest in its European birthplace.

Q How come animals don't starve when they hibernate?

A They binge, then go comatose. Does this sound like something that's happened to you after you polished off a quart of Häagen-Dazs? Can you imagine that food coma lasting all winter?

Animals that hibernate have triggers that warn them to glut themselves for the winter ahead. As the days get shorter and colder, the critters' internal clocks—which mark time through fluctuations of hormones, neurotransmitters, and amino acids—tell them to fill up and shut down. Bingeing is important; if these creatures don't build up enough fat, they won't survive. The fat that they store for hibernation is brown (rather than white, like human body fat) and collects near the brain, heart, and lungs.

Animals have a number of reasons for hibernating. Cold-blooded creatures such as snakes and turtles adjust their body temperatures according to the weather; in winter, their blood runs so cold that many of their bodily functions essentially stop. Warm-blooded rodents can more easily survive the extreme chills of winter, but they have a different problem: finding food. They most likely developed their ability to hibernate as a way of surviving winter's dearth of munchies.

After an animal has heeded the biological call to pig out, its metabolism starts to slow down. As it hibernates, some bodily functions—digestion, the immune system—shut down altogether. Its heartbeat slows to ten or fewer beats per minute, and its senses stop registering sounds and smells. The animal's body consumes much less fuel than normal—its metabolism can be as low as 1 percent of its normal rate. The stored fat, then, is enough to satisfy the minimal demands of the animal's body, provided the creature found enough to eat in the fall and is otherwise healthy.

It can take hours or even days for the animal's body temperature to rise back to normal after it awakens from hibernation. But time is of the essence—the beast desperately needs water, and thirst drives it out of its nest. However, the animal is groggy and slow of foot—it walks like a drunk—so it can be easy prey if it doesn't hydrate quickly.

Which animals hibernate? Small ones, mostly—cold-blooded and warm-blooded critters alike. The first category includes snakes, lizards, frogs, and tortoises; the second includes dormice, hedge-hogs, skunks, and bats.

But what about the bear, the animal that is most closely associated with hibernation? Here's a shocker: Bears don't hibernate. They slow down, sleep a lot, and lose weight during winter, but they don't truly hibernate. So if you're ever taking a peaceful nature walk on a sunny winter morn, beware. A bear might be out there.

Q How much rain does it take to make a rain forest?

A It takes eighty inches of rain per year to make a rain forest, but the scientists who categorize these things aren't picky. There should be no feelings of inadequacy among forests whose drops per annum don't quite make the cut; if a wooded area has a rate of precipitation that comes close to the eighty-inch mark, it will most likely be taken into the fold.

Rain falls about ninety days per year in a rain forest. As much as 50 percent of this precipitation evaporates, meaning that rain forests recycle their water supply. In non-rain forest areas, water evaporates and is transported (via clouds) to different regions. In a rain forest, however, the unique climate and weather patterns often cause the precipitation to fall over the same area from which it evaporated.

A rain forest is comprised of evergreen trees, either broadleaf or coniferous, and other types of intense vegetation. These regions collectively contain more than two-thirds of the plant species on the planet. There are two types of rain forests: tropical and temperate. Tropical rain forests are located near the equator; temperate rain forests crop up near oceanic coastlines, particularly where mountain ranges focus rainfall on a particular region.

Rain forests can be found on every continent except Antarctica. The largest tropical rain forest is the Amazon in South America; the largest temperate rain forest is in the Pacific Northwest, stretching from northern California all the way to Alaska.

At one time, rain forests covered as much as 14 percent of the earth, but that number is now down to about 6 percent. Scientists estimate that an acre and a half of rain forest—the equivalent of a little more than a football field—is lost every second. The trees are taken for lumber, and the land is tilled for farming. At that rate, scientists estimate, rain forests will disappear completely within the next forty years—and it will take a lot more than eighty inches of rain per year to bring them back.

Q How terrible was Ivan the Terrible?

A About as cruel and terrible as anyone could be. It's pretty hard to whitewash the reputation of a man who murdered friends, tortured enemies, and beat his own son to death.

Ivan IV became ruler of Russia in 1533 at the tender age of three, after his father died. His mother was a regent; her family and other nobles—called boyars—fought each other often and violently for control of the government. Ivan grew to hate them. His tutors were monks, and he learned an intolerant brand of Christianity that stayed with him his whole life.

In 1547, while still a teenager, Ivan had himself crowned the first *tsar*—a word meaning "God's anointed." That's how he thought of himself. He made pilgrimages, built churches, and fancied himself chosen by God to hold absolute power—including the power to torture or kill anyone who disagreed with him.

In the early part of his reign, Ivan was not a bad ruler. He called consultative assemblies, issued a new law code, reformed local governments, and conquered some Tatar states. His first marriage was happy and lasted more than twelve years. But after his first wife died—he was married seven times—Ivan started behaving like a sadistic lunatic and earned his nickname, "the Terrible."

Convinced that his beloved wife had been poisoned by the hated boyars, Ivan attacked the people of that class by seizing their lands and executing them whenever he decided they were traitors. He also turned on old friends and advisors and had the highest-ranking church official in Moscow murdered. His most shocking crime was the murder of his own son and heir, Ivan, in 1581. He beat his adult son in front of the young man's wife, then delivered the death blow with an iron-pointed staff.

Ivan held power longer than any other Russian ruler. After Ivan died in 1584, his feeble-minded son, Feodor, took over because he was the infamous despot's last remaining heir. An autopsy done centuries after his death revealed that Ivan's spine had been fused by disease, probably causing intense pain, which experts say may explain part of his insane behavior. But only part.

Q How many ants make a full meal for a giant anteater?

A How many ants would an anteater eat if an anteater could eat ants? How about a whopping thirty-five thousand per day? And when the giant anteater can't eat ants, it will settle for termites and consume about an equal number.

That sounds like an awful lot of insects, but keep in mind that the average ant or termite weighs only three milligrams. So despite the volume of insects that it eats, the voracious anteater is consuming less than an ounce of food at every meal. Fortunately, the anteater's metabolism is very slow. Anteaters typically maintain a body temperature of only 90.9 degrees Fahrenheit—one of the lowest temps in the animal kingdom—which enables them to thrive on this highly specialized diet.

How do they eat? After locating a large nest of ants or termites, an anteater gouges a hole with its powerful front claws, pokes its nose in, and starts chowing down. Its long, snaky tongue is the ideal utensil for scooping up those tiny ants. Coated with sticky black hairs, the tongue extends more than two feet from the anteater's mouth and flicks in and out at the amazing rate of one hundred fifty times a minute. Because it lacks teeth, the anteater also uses its tongue to crush the ants against the roof of its mouth before swallowing.

Why do anteaters eat ants, anyway? According to zoologists, anteaters cannot produce the gastric juices that other mammals use to digest food. Ants and termites are highly acidic and decompose easily in the anteater's stomach without additional acids.

Incidentally, anteaters in zoos enjoy a more varied diet, with occasional fruits, vegetables, and honey. But their keepers must make sure they receive the right balance of acid, or the anteaters will not survive.

A full-grown giant anteater is a hefty creature, measuring about four feet high from ground to shoulder and five to seven feet long from nose to tail. Adult males weigh up to ninety pounds, females a little less than that. Anteaters are native to South America. Their primary habitat is east of the Andes Mountains in northwest Argentina and parts of Uruguay.

Though they rarely threaten humans, anteaters have often been hunted for sport and are presently considered endangered by the International Union for Conservation of Nature. Anteaters are excellent conservationists. An anteater will never clean out an entire ant nest at a single sitting. It will always leave enough ants to allow the colony to regenerate, thus ensuring a future meal.

These are pretty smart tactics for a creature with a fairly small brain. Maybe some big-brained mammals should follow the anteater's example and make sure to conserve their own natural resources as wisely.

Q How come I yawn?

A Chances are good that at some point as you peruse this book, you'll break out into a yawn. It's not because you're anything less than riveted, although it might help if you're a little bored. A yawn is simply one of nature's irresistible urges. Why? Ask a doctor who has spent years studying the structure and function of the human body, and after much theorizing, you'll probably get a dressed-up version of "I dunno."

There are many theories for why we yawn—and why we pandiculate, which is when we stretch and yawn at the same time—but they have holes as gaping as the mouth of an unrepentant yawner.

One theory is that we yawn to expel a buildup of carbon dioxide from our lungs—that the yawn is a maneuver that lets the body take in a larger-than-usual amount of oxygen and displace excess carbon dioxide. But if this were the only reason for a yawn, people who already have enough oxygen would never do it. Studies have demonstrated that increasing the amount of oxygen or decreasing the amount of carbon dioxide in a room does not decrease the frequency of yawns.

Even if it's not entirely satisfying, the oxygen/carbon dioxide theory can be tied to another popular explanation for the phenomenon: boredom and fatigue. When we're tired or bored, we begin to take breaths that are shallower, so it would make sense that we'd need the occasional influx of extra oxygen. But why, then, are yawns contagious? Fifty-five percent of people yawn when they see someone else do it; for many, even thinking or reading about yawning will cause it.

Yet another theory contends that the yawn is a vestigial habit that has been passed down to us from our distant ancestors—a relic that shows how humans communicated before developing language. Perhaps we yawned to intimidate by showing our teeth or as another kind of signal to our fellow humans. Yawning could have been a means of synchronizing a group as it passed from person to person. A similar explanation suggests that yawning actually increases alertness, which could help explain why yawning is contagious—the more alert a group, the more effective it is at fighting or hunting.

There are also theories that yawning helps cool the brain, keeps the lungs from collapsing, and helps equalize ear pressure. Whatever the reason we yawn, it is certainly ingrained in us from an early age: Fetuses begin yawning at eleven weeks. And unless an eleven-week-old fetus is thoughtful enough to be bored, there's got to be something more to yawning than that.

Q How does scratch-and-sniff stuff work?

A The basic idea is simple: Manufacturers encase tiny drops of scented oil in thin polymer membranes and stick millions of these little bitty capsules to a piece of paper or a sticker. When you scratch the paper, your fingernail breaks open the tiny capsules and the scented oil (along with its smell) spills out. And there you have it—instant banana odor.

The manufacturing process—called microencapsulation—is a little more complicated. To whip up a batch of scratch-and-sniff stuff, manufacturers combine scented oil and a solution of water and a polymer compound in a big vat. The oil and the solution won't mix, just like oil and vinegar in vinaigrette salad dressing won't mix. But when a giant blending machine stirs everything, the oil breaks down into millions of tiny drops that are suspended in the polymer solution. You see the same effect when you shake a bottle of vinaigrette.

Next, the manufacturer adds a catalyst chemical to the mix that reacts with the polymer and changes its behavior. While before it was soluble (it dissolved in water), in its new form it becomes insoluble (it doesn't mix with water). In other words, the polymer separates from the water and turns into a solid. As it solidifies, it forms shells around the tiny oil droplets. The manufacturer dries these capsules and mixes them into a slurry so that they can be applied to scratch-and-sniff strips.

It's yet another example of how science is being put to good use and making the world a better place for one and all.

Q How did I get my birthmark?

A In the old days, you would have gone to your mother with some questions. While pregnant with you, did she: Spill wine on herself? Get an X-ray? Suffer a terrible fright? Eat excessive amounts of beets, watermelons, or strawberries?

She did? Well, that sure is interesting. But spilled wine, an X-ray, a scary incident, or an excessive consumption of beets, watermelons, or strawberries is not the reason for your birthmark, although many people—including a few prominent doctors—used to think it was. Truth is, the causes of most birthmarks are unknown. We do, however, know how the two major types of birthmarks—vascular and pigmented—physically form.

Vascular birthmarks—such as macular stains, port-wine stains, and hemangiomas—happen when blood vessels get bunched together, tangled, or just don't grow normally. Pigmented birthmarks—such as café-au-lait spots, Mongolian spots, and congenital moles—form when an overgrowth of cells creates extra pigment on the skin.

Like we said, the experts insist that birthmarks are not caused by what your mother did, craved, ate, or wished for during her pregnancy. Furthermore, they can't be prevented. This earth-shaking news affects a whole lot of people: Up to a third of newborns have some kind of colorful spot, mark, mole, blemish, or blotch. Think of them as nature's tattoos.

Whether brown, red, pink, black, blue, or purple, most birthmarks are harmless. Some will shrink on their own over time. Others can be removed with surgery or the zap of a laser. The rest are permanent fixtures.

If you have a birthmark, don't waste time worrying about it. Instead, you should consider yourself special. Depending on the old wife with whom you consult, it could well be the sign of an angel's kiss or even a battle wound from a previous life. How's that for a mark of honor?

Q How important must you be to be considered assassinated?

A Here's a question that popped up while we were working on our latest JFK conspiracy theory. (Did you know that there was a UFO spotted in North Dakota—heading due south— two days before Kennedy's assassination? You didn't, did you?) There's no question in the popular mind that JFK was assassinated, as were Presidents Lincoln, Garfield, and McKinley. But assassinations aren't limited to politicians—they can happen to activists (Martin Luther King) and even to musicians (John Lennon). How is it decided who's assassinated and who's just plain murdered?

For the answer, we need to first look at the definition and deriva- tion of the word itself, and for that we turn to our trusty *Oxford English Dictionary*. The word "assassin," according to the *OED*, is derived from the Arabic word *hashshashin*, which was the name of a secretive sect known for the skillful killing of its political en- emies. According to legend, members of the sect enjoyed a little pre-assassination toking of the hash pipe (hence the name). Though this legend is probably not rooted in truth, you'd be forgiven if, after looking at the mug shots of Mark David Chapman (who assassinated Lennon), James Earl Ray (King), and Lee Harvey Oswald (JFK, unless you believe in conspiracy theories), you imagined that they, too, partook in a little pre-treachery smoke.

The political nature of the hashshashin's killing is reinforced by the *OED*'s definition of assassinate: "to kill by treacherous violence." Treachery, of course, indicates a certain amount of plotting and betrayal, and is often used in a political sense, but doesn't neces- sarily have to be. (Aliens from outer space, for example, with their advanced intelligence and technology, are more than capable of intricate plotting and treachery.)

There seem to be three main criteria, then, to be considered assassinated: (1) the victim must be well known, (2) he or she must have a political bent, and (3) he or she must be the victim of treachery and plotting. This helps explain why Lennon's shooting by Chapman is often referred to as an assassination and, say, the tragic death of Marvin Gaye (he was shot by his father at his Los Angeles home) is not. Lennon was certainly a political figure, if not a politician per se—the FBI kept a file detailing the former Beatle's rabble-rousing. Gaye, on the other hand, was simply a singer, albeit one with a social conscience. Now, back to that JFK conspiracy theory...

Q How do restaurants make money from all-you-can-eat buffets?

A Go holler, "Feast!" and watch the egg rolls fly. Behold the buffet, humankind's magnificent shrine to bountiful banquets and conspicuous crapulence, all for a nominal fee. But while watching the masses devour heaping helpings of food from king-size self-serve stations is a compelling spectacle, it's equally remarkable to discover that some restaurants profit from this bargain-price gluttony.

How so? It starts with labor costs. Servers at all-you-can-eat restaurants don't have to take orders and deliver food; all that is needed are people to clear plates from the table, fill drinks (this task isn't even necessary at restaurants that have self-serve drink stations), and replenish the buffet. This means that fewer employees can tend to more tables, and those tables turn over more quickly than at a normal restaurant because there is no wait for food—it's an equation that contributes to the financial success of all-you-can-eat establishments.

Menu options are another factor. Quantity, not quality, is king in the buffet line—in other words, you're not going to find haute cuisine at Old Country Buffet. Some dollars may be lost when diners go nuts on the more costly dishes, like meat and seafood, but that deficit is counterbalanced by the people who fill up on the bounty of less expensive fare, such as potatoes and other starches. Besides, restaurants have some tricks to guard against overindulgence, such as providing smaller plates and utensils, and pre-plating meat and seafood items. Who knew the buffet game was so sneaky?

Pricing proves to be the trickiest part of the equation. A restaurateur must measure the cost of serving each dish against the amount that is consumed. These numbers yield a usage history and enable the restaurant owner to calculate future costs and revenue. As is the case with just about everything these days, restaurateurs can use computer software to determine their various food formulas.

Thanks to a program called EatecNetX, a veritable feast of information—such as how many servings of an item were prepared on a given day, how many were consumed, and even what time the dish ran out—is merely a few keystrokes away. So is important minutia, like how much of various ingredients needs to be on hand in the kitchen to prepare a certain number of servings of a dish.

It isn't all chicken wings and smiles in the buffet biz. In their quest to uphold the bottom line, some restaurant owners have ruled their buffets with an iron fist, denying certain customers service, asking others to leave after reaching a designated food limit, or tacking extra charges onto bills. These don't seem like wise practices, considering the all-you-can-eat business is predicated on allowing customers to stuff their faces with impunity. No one goes to a buffet to eat, drink, and be wary.

Q How come you can't wear white after Labor Day?

A All good GRITS (girls raised in the South) know that you're not supposed to wear white after Labor Day—or before Easter Sunday. It's what their mamas taught them. It's a Southern tradition. And in the South, you don't mess with tradition.

Does that mean the no-white rule originated below the Mason-Dixon Line? Fashion etiquette does trend a bit more formal in this section of the United States. It's a region where upbringing, social skills, and unspoken rules have always been central to living the genteel life. And Southern belles know bad manners when they see them.

Just imagine their horror when the nouveau riche in the late nineteenth century began showing up at tea parties and cotillions in the middle of October wearing snowy, milky, unpigmented garments. They probably didn't carry proper parasols either. Goodness gracious.

Though we can't be certain, it is conceivable the no-white-after-Labor-Day rule was an edict handed down by members of long-standing society families. They were quite concerned about the fashion etiquette of those who lacked the experience, finesse, and good taste of old money, so they established specific codified guidelines for the newbies. (By the way, don't even think about wearing velvet after Valentine's Day.)

What's the point of a seasonal style statute? For Southern ladies, it may still be about honoring heritage and showing respect. For the rest of us, it's a simple reminder to put warm-weather fabrics like seersucker and linen away for the winter.

Fashion authorities say it's perfectly okay, if not stylish, to wear white year-round, especially in a temperate climate. Not convinced? Emily Post—the most trusted name in etiquette—says: "The old rule about wearing white only between Memorial Day and Labor Day is a thing of the past. Today the question of wearing white applies to the weight of the fabrics, not color."

So don't wear a white eyelet sundress to Christmas dinner. And please—please!—put away the bright white pumps. Diann Catlin, an etiquette consultant from Jacksonville, Florida, says it's not white clothes that are a no-no after Labor Day—it's white shoes. Whatever the rule, tennis players and brides are exempt.

Q How does salt melt ice?

A The link between salt and hypertension is clear. Yet each winter-highway departments dump billions of tons of salt onto the nation's frozen highways, with complete disregard for the health of the nation's transportation arteries. Is it any wonder that our highways are pitted with potholes? More importantly, has anybody considered the link between salt on the highways and the increase in incidents of road rage?

Until somebody tackles these really important questions, we'll have to satisfy ourselves with the explanation for why all that salt gets dumped in the first place. No, it's not to add a savory zing to the roads—it's to melt the ice. But in order to understand how salt melts ice, we'll need to take a trip back to chemistry class, where we learned how water freezes.

Water, as we all know, is known chemically as H_2O—it's two hydrogen atoms and one oxygen atom that bind together to form a molecule. These molecules are always bouncing about, though this movement is contingent on temperature. Heat speeds up the movement of molecules; cold slows it down. Eventually, if the temperature gets cold enough, water molecules cling together to form ice. As even we chemistry dummies know, this happens at thirty-two degrees Fahrenheit.

In order to melt ice, either the air temperature needs to go up (a sunny day, for example) or the freezing point of the water itself must be lowered to below thirty-two degrees. Enter salt. When salt is dumped onto ice, the salt molecules bind with the water molecules; as a result, a colder temperature is required for the salt and water molecules to break apart so that ice can be formed.

However, this process requires that some water be present—if the temperature is too cold, there won't be any liquid water molecules to which the salt molecules can bind. (This is why in especially cold climates, highway trucks sometimes dump sand onto roadways—sand doesn't bind with water, but it does provide better traction.)

This principle is applied in other fields as well. In culinary school, chefs are taught that adding salt to water raises the temperature at which water boils, and the same idea is behind how antifreeze keeps your engine from freezing or locking up in the winter.

It's tempting to think that this would work with the human body as well: A couple of teaspoons of salt should warm you up, right? We don't recommend it. Though salt may theoretically warm your heart, it will probably wear it out, too.

Q How can a bell save you?

A "Saved by the bell" is a phrase that's uttered in times of great relief, when something intervenes at the very moment all hope seems lost. For example: An unprepared student is stuttering and searching for a response to the teacher's question, then sighs thankfully as he hears the end-of-period bell. But where did this phrase originate?

Probably boxing, in which a bell is rung at the beginning and the end of each round. Sportswriters began using the phrase toward the end of the nineteenth century to describe a boxer who had been beaten to a pulp but was saved, at least temporarily, from certain annihilation by the clanging of the end-of-round bell.

There is another, more interesting potential origin of the phrase, although it has little basis in fact. It goes something like this: In medieval times, folks drank from lead cups. Their drinks would become contaminated by the toxic metal, and when the revelers passed out, they would go into a so-called lead coma. To doctors of the day, with their limited knowledge and medical equipment, these people appeared to be dead. So, accordingly, they were sealed in wooden coffins and buried. Discovery of these mistakes came much later, when the coffins were dug up and examined. The inside lids were marked with deep scratches from the prematurely buried, who had desperately tried to break out.

Such incidents fostered a fear of being buried alive and led to the invention of the "safety coffin." This puppy came with a tube, which protruded from the surface of the gravesite and attached to the lid. A bell was located at the top of the tube; a string hung down so that, upon awakening, the not-quite-deceased could ring the bell and be saved.

Research shows that the safety coffin really did exist; a record of the 1868 patent request by Franz Vester of New Jersey for this lifesaver is reproduced in the book *Mad Inventions*. However, there's no evidence that any bell-ringing actually occurred.

So if you want accuracy regarding the origin of the phrase in question, look to the boxing ring. But if you want a great story, take a gander at the safety coffin.

Q How many kids have found razor blades in their candy apples?

 A Halloween, All Hallows Eve, Samhain. Whatever you call it, October 31 is the night a kid's dreams come true. Not only do children get to dress up in costumes, but they also get to stand on their neighbors' porches and collect candy.

But it's not all fun and games. Parents are cautioned yearly to never allow their children to eat unwrapped candy that is collected on Halloween night. Whenever a child gets sick in early November and there's even the slightest chance that the illness is related to eating tainted candy, alarmist news stations call for parents to dump everything their children brought home. While these reports might be broadcast with the best of intentions—ensuring the safety of our children—almost all of them wind up being false alarms.

Sociologists refer this as the "myth of the Halloween sadist." It's been causing yearly widespread panic since at least the 1970s, when a child died from an overdose of heroin that was said to have been given to him via Halloween candy. (This turned out to be untrue; the heroin belonged to an uncle, and it was hidden away in the kid's Halloween loot by family members in an attempt to keep the uncle out of jail.) Since then, similar incidents have occurred, and in nearly every case, Halloween candy hasn't turned out to be the offender.

There have been more cases of foreign objects in Halloween goods than of tainted candy. In the late 1960s, New Jersey saw a rash of apples that did indeed have razor blades inserted into them—enough to warrant state legislative action on the topic—but few of the cases involved actual injury. The most notable case of tampering occurred in 2000, when a man put needles in Snickers bars and handed them out to neighborhood children. No one, however, was seriously hurt.

The myth of dangerous candy persists today partly due to young pranksters. By taking candy that has been collected (say, your little brother's stash) and inserting something mildly dangerous, the prankster spooks an entire neighborhood and gets a good laugh. Urban legend debunker and sociologist Joel Best reports one such case, in which a child approached his parents with a candy bar that was sprinkled with ant poison.

The child, it turned out, did the sprinkling. It was good for a quick laugh, maybe, but these kinds of pranks perpetuate the notion that Halloween is a night for real parental fear.

Q How come the pope changes his name upon taking office?

A Think of it as a safety measure to ensure that the papacy remains classy. The tradition started in the year 533: The Catholic Church had just selected a new pope whose given name was Mercurius, a reference to Mercury, the Roman god of commerce. After centuries of stamping out paganism, having a pope named after a pagan god wouldn't do. So Mercurius became John II.

Over the next several centuries, a few other popes changed their names, but these were exceptions rather than the rule. It wasn't until the year 1009 that name-changing became the "in" thing. That's when a pope who had an unfortunate name was chosen: Pietro Osporci. His first name just wouldn't work, since it was derived from that of Saint Peter, Prince of Apostles and Pontiff *Numero Uno*. (No pope has ever taken this name, because none would compare himself to Saint Peter.) Even worse, Osporci means "pig's snout," so that was no good, either. He chose a more dignified moniker, Sergius IV, and changing names was established as a standard practice. Since then, only two popes—Hadrian VI and Marcellus II, both in the sixteenth century—have kept their birth names.

The practice of taking on a new name can have a spiritual dimension as well. In the Old Testament, for example, an angel defeats Jacob in a wrestling match, demonstrating the sovereignty of God; he then gives Jacob the name Israel, meaning "God commands." And the New Testament tells the story of a man named Simon whom Jesus renamed Peter (and who eventually became Saint Peter) when he became a disciple. In this way, a name change can signify the beginning of a new spiritual life, often in an elevated position.

And what position could be more elevated than the pope's? This may be why renaming is one of the first orders of business after a new pope is selected. As soon as the elected pope accepts the position, the Dean of the College of Cardinals asks him, "*Quomodo vis vocari?*" ("By what name do you wish to be called?")

There's no *Big Book of Pope Names* to consult, but new popes generally name themselves after their predecessors or saints they hope to emulate. For example, the current pope said this about his choice of Benedict XVI: "Firstly, I remember Pope Benedict XV, that courageous prophet of peace, who guided the Church through turbulent times of war. In his footsteps, I place my ministry in the service of reconciliation and harmony between peoples. Additionally, I recall Saint Benedict of Nursia, co-patron of Europe, whose life evokes the Christian roots of Europe. I ask him to help us all to hold firm to the centrality of Christ in our Christian life: May Christ always take first place in our thoughts and actions."

The name may not be as cool as Pope Awesome the First, but it has a nice ring to it.

Q How exactly do you cut mustard?

A We've seen enough movies to know how to cut to the chase. Our parents taught us how to cut the crap, and we've spent all our lives cutting it close. We even know how to cut the cheese (much to the dismay of our colleagues). But we have no idea how anyone can cut mustard, nor do we know why we would want to.

The phrase "cut the mustard"—meaning to be up to standard or, if we may invoke another bizarre phrase, "up to snuff"—is a fairly recent entry in the idiomatic lexicon. But how and where it originated is up for debate. Most lexicographers credit the short-story writer O. Henry with first using the phrase in print in 1902, though there are reports of earlier popular employment.

Several schools of thought have emerged regarding the phrase's origin. The first asserts that "cutting the mustard" doesn't have anything to do with mustard at all. Instead, the "mustard" in question is a misappropriation of the military term "muster," which is a gathering of soldiers for inspection. Passing muster, as any recruit can tell you, is the same thing as cutting the mustard. But this seemingly plausible explanation loses credence when one realizes that the phrase "cutting the mustard" doesn't appear in any old military documents or literature—and there's no evidence that "cutting the muster" was used prior to 1902.

A second theory holds that "cutting the mustard" evokes a literal act of cutting—not of the condiment itself, but of that from which the condiment is derived: the mustard seed. This tasty seed is very small and is protected by a hard shell, which would make cutting the mustard a difficult task—one that would earn the cutter the same approval that would be bestowed on someone who cuts the mustard in a figurative way. Of course, cutting mustard seeds individually would be idiotic—the preferred method of processing is crushing the seeds into a powder. But nobody in his or her right mind would ever use the phrase "pulverize the mustard." Making mustard this way isn't much of a challenge, for one thing (and the phrase doesn't exactly roll off the tongue).

According to yet another explanation, "cutting the mustard" refers to the act of adding vinegar to mustard powder during the production of condiment-grade mustard in order to soften the spice's inherent bitterness and make it more palatable. But if you're metaphorically cutting the mustard, you aren't mellowing an acrid flavor in some way—or even improving anything. It's hard to see how this usage explains the colloquial meaning of the idiom, which makes this theory as unlikely as the others we have mentioned.

The final school of thought argues that although the phrase "cut the mustard" is relatively new, it is rooted in a far older tradition, in which mustard was an emblem of panache and pizzazz. As far back as the mid-seventeenth century, English scribes claimed that enthusiastic young go-getters were "keen as mustard." Why?

Probably because mustard played a key role in British cuisine—it was one of the few affordable spices that could enliven the country's dismal meat-and-potatoes fare. As a result, mustard became associated with zest. When the word "mustard" was combined with "cut"—as in "he cuts a fine figure" or "he's a cut above"—a phrase that evokes proven excellence may have been born.

But let's cut to the chase: No one has found a cut-and-dried origin of the term. This can only mean one thing: Etymologists haven't been cutting the mustard.

Q How come there's not a channel one on your television?

Man came by to hook up my cable TV
We settled in for the night, my baby and me
We switched 'round and 'round 'til half-past dawn
There was fifty-seven channels and nothin' on
—Bruce Springsteen, "57 Channels (And Nothin' On)"

A Have you ever wondered which programs Bruce Springsteen saw in 1992 as he surfed the channels available on his newly installed cable? Was it the smarmy cast of *L.A. Law* that so repulsed him? Or was it the predictable mystery of *Matlock* that pushed him over the edge? Or perhaps the vampiric visage of Ron Popeil? This is a question for philosophers to debate; we'll probably never know the answer. But there's one thing that we can say for sure: In all of his channel flipping, the Boss never took a look at channel one—he couldn't have. Channels start at two and go up from there.

It wasn't always this way. The American television industry took off in April 1941, when two stations began to broadcast from New York: WNBT (later NBC) and WCBW (later CBS); they used channels one and two, respectively. Within a year, the nation had four television stations that reached more than ten thousand households—and channel one was a going concern.

But World War II brought the fledgling medium to a grinding halt. For the next several years, the country devoted its resources to more pressing needs. By the time commercial broadcasting was ready to resume in 1946, new technological developments had changed both radio and television. Competition for the airwaves was fierce—stations could broadcast farther, faster, and on higher frequencies than ever before.

Everyone wanted a piece of the big pie in the sky. A series of congressional hearings were held to apportion the broadcast spectrum, and by 1947, the Federal Communications Commission (FCC) had awarded a total of thirteen channels to the television networks. Channel one was designated a community channel for stations with limited broadcasting range because it had the lowest frequency.

But there was trouble in this television paradise. As the number of broadcasters increased, the airwaves began to get crowded, especially in larger metropolitan areas. Frequencies started to overlap, causing chaos and complaints when viewers found their quiz shows scrambled with the nightly news, or vice versa.

The FCC took steps to reduce this interference. In 1948, the organization decided to free up space by disallowing broadcasts on the lowest frequency—channel one. That bandwidth would instead be devoted to mobile land services—operations like two-way radio communication in taxicabs. Commercial television retained channels two through twelve. When the FCC's plan went into effect, television manufacturers simply dispensed with the one on the tuning dial; the millions of people who bought their first television sets in the 1950s barely even noticed its absence.

Since then, our options for televised entertainment have multiplied at a staggering rate. Bruce Springsteen's fifty-seven-channel cable package sounds quaint to contemporary subscribers who have hundreds of stations and a TiVO to record them all. But even with this nearly unlimited number of channels available in our living rooms, we'll never again have a channel one. As to whether there's anything on? We'll leave that up to you—and Bruce.

Q How is it that we don't see baby pigeons?

A If you aren't seeing baby pigeons, you're just looking in the wrong places. Until they're ready to take flight, the young birds hang out in nests while their moms and dads are out socializing.

Pigeons, those head-bobbing city slickers that so often repaint statues and other objects of their "affection," are descended from rock doves, which got their name from their propensity for building their nests on the craggy faces of cliffs. When the rock dove population spills into a metropolitan area—or when an ever-expanding metropolitan area infringes on rock dove territory—the birds build their nests on the unnatural ledges and shelves of tall buildings and bridges.

Baby pigeons, known as squabs, stay in their nests until they are able to fly. Obviously, squabs are as common as adult pigeons. They're just not as visible—unless you're a window washer.

Q How much wood can a woodchuck chuck?

A "How much wood would a woodchuck chuck, if a woodchuck could chuck wood?" This classic tongue twister has been part of the English lexicon for ages. But has anybody really thought about what it means? Has anybody even seen a woodchuck chucking wood? Or chucking anything, for that matter?

Part of the confusion lies in the origin of the word "woodchuck." A woodchuck (*Marmota monax*) is, in fact, the same thing as a groundhog. In the Appalachians, it's known as a whistle pig. According to etymologists, the word woodchuck is probably derived from early colonial British settlers who bastardized *wuchak*, the local Native American word for groundhog. Because many early Americans couldn't be bothered to learn languages other than English (sort of like present-day Americans), they simply transformed the Algonquian word into one that sounded like English. That the name made absolutely no sense mattered little to these settlers, who were far more concerned with issues like starvation and massive epidemics of fatal illnesses.

Still, the question remains. What if woodchucks could chuck wood? Not surprisingly, there is little research on the topic. Indeed, no studies as of yet have proved that woodchucks are even capable of chucking wood, though there is ample evidence that woodchucks enjoy gnawing through wood when they encounter it.

There is, however, one thing that woodchucks are adept at chucking: dirt. The average woodchuck is quite a burrower, building complicated underground bunkers that would have made Saddam Hussein envious. These tunnels have been known to reach more than forty-five feet in length with depths of several feet. Based on these measurements, one woodchuck expert determined that if the displaced dirt in a typical burrow was replaced with wood, the average whistle pig might be able chuck about seven hundred pounds of it.

In the end, the best answer is probably provided by the rhyme itself. "How much wood would a woodchuck chuck, if a woodchuck could chuck wood? A woodchuck would chuck all the wood he could, if a woodchuck could chuck wood." Which would probably be none.

Q How can a penny be bad?

A Pennies may be lucky, but they certainly aren't bad. In the aphorism "A bad penny always turns up," the penny is standing in for a person. It's a way of saying a scoundrel will keep coming back no matter how many times he's sent away.

The saying originated in England, where men were sometimes referred to as shillings, an allusion to the amount per day an enlisted man was paid to serve the crown. A "bad shilling" was a man who was lazy, incompetent, or immoral. When this aphorism made the transatlantic jump from England to America, so did the language of the currency—and "bad shilling" became "bad penny."

The saying is also related to the phrase "taking the king's shilling," which dates to 1707. To take the king's shilling was to enlist in the military. Comparing men to money dates back to the ancient Romans: "Soldier" comes from *solidus*, which was the gold coin that enlisted men were given as compensation.

American soldiers have never been paid in pennies, and American people have never been referred to as pennies, but the phrase— like the penny to which it refers—turns up from time to time.

Q How many people bought a Pet Rock?

A At least 1.3 million by Christmas morning, 1975. And that figure counts only the original Pet Rocks. In the months before Christmas, thousands of cheaper imitations were also sold, and no one can guess how many of those changed hands.

Gary Dahl, the marketing genius who thought up the Pet Rock, got the idea from listening to his friends complain about their trouble-some pets. He persuaded a former boss to back him financially and arranged to haul two and a half tons of pebbles from Rosarita

Beach in Mexico to his Northern California headquarters. After packaging them in carrying crates filled with nesting straw and cut with air holes, he introduced the Pet Rock at gift shows that autumn.

Soon he was shipping thousands of rocks per day to stores such as Neiman-Marcus and Macy's. Dahl earned ninety-five cents for every authentic Pet Rock sold at $3.95. He became a millionaire three weeks before Christmas, appeared on TV talk shows, and was written up in *Newsweek, People,* and many major newspapers.

Why? What sparked such an insane fad? Dahl took a stab at explaining it, saying, "I think the country was depressed and needed a giggle." He was probably right, because for most people, the real fun of having a Pet Rock was reading the manual. Written by Dahl and titled *The Care and Training of Your PET ROCK,* the thirty-two-page booklet described how to teach your new pet basic commands such as "Stay," "Sit," and "Play dead." Although rocks learned these tricks quickly, more complicated commands such as "Come" required "extraordinary patience" from the trainer.

Nostalgic attempts to recreate the magic—or take it a step further with Rock Concerts or Rock Families (often with googly eyes glued onto the rocks)—fell flat. In 2000, Pet Rocks were packaged and sold with minimal changes to the original design. One noticeable omission in the 2000 version of the manual was the "Attack" command. In 1975, owners were told that when confronted by a mugger, they should, "Reach into your pocket or purse [and] extract your pet rock. Shout the command, ATTACK. And bash the mugger's head in." Presumably, the twenty-first century is too litigious to give this advice to rock owners.

None of the redux sales strategies worked. Pet Rocks enjoyed their fifteen minutes of fame, but after their initial—and legendary— success, all attempts to remarket Pet Rocks have dropped like a stone.

Q How can wine be dry if it's a liquid?

A Okay, we admit it: The Q&A staff isn't the most cultured bunch. (You've probably already ascertained as much.) We'll happily trade the caviar for a good burger and take a pass on the opera if there's football on TV. The closest we get to champagne is grabbing a six-pack of Miller High Life—"the champagne of beers"—on the way home from work. If we drink wine at all, it's out of a box with a tap.

Part of the reason most people feel intimidated by wine culture is the vocabulary—and the implied snobbery—that surrounds it. Terms like "bouquet," "tannins," "finish," and "body" don't seem like they should have much to do with anything you drink. And only in the most wine-drenched state of illogic would the term "dry" have anything to do with a liquid. Yet it is a word that oenophiles use with impunity.

For those whose experience with wine is limited to Bartles & Jaymes commercials, a quick primer on wine tasting might be illuminative. There are literally hundreds of wine terms, but they describe just a handful of qualities: how wine looks (clarity and color), smells (aroma and bouquet), feels in the mouth (body), tastes (balance, acidity, and notes), and tastes after swallowing (finish). These are dependant on an array of variables, like which grapes are used, where the grapes are grown, and how the wine is stored.

Most wines are made in a similar way. After the grapes are harvested, they are put into a crusher that extracts the juice and separates the stems and skins. The color of the wine depends not on the color of the grape—all grape juice is clear—but on how much contact between the grape juice and the grape skin is allowed. (The stems and skins give red wine its color.) Yeast is then added to the juice/skin mixture; this yeast feeds on the sugars in the juice, which starts the fermentation process.

The sweetness of a wine depends on a number of factors, including the type of grape that is used to make it. When a wine has a noticeable amount of sugar, connoisseurs say that it is sweet. And if it doesn't have much sugar? Connoisseurs don't call it sour, that's for sure—instead, they say it's dry.

Making things all the more confusing, "dry" sometimes refers to the abundance of tannins in a wine rather than its relative sweetness. Tannins are bitter compounds that are found in grape stems, seeds, and skins, and they impart a mouth-puckering quality to wines. Wine that has a lot of tannins can make you feel as if moisture is being leeched out of your mouth. The result? Your mouth gets "dry."

In the end, it might be better to leave all of the wine talk to the oenophiles. We'll stick to what we know—and that's beer. The beauty of beer is its simplicity. After all, you need only one word to describe it: good.

Q How does the cat get out of the bag?

A If you've let the cat out of the bag, you've divulged a secret—you've probably ruined what was supposed to be Aunt Miriam's surprise sixtieth birthday party. But just what do cats and bags have to do with spilling the beans?

The origin of this feline-related phrase likely dates to medieval England in the fifteen hundreds. Back then, it was common for merchants to sell goods such as produce and livestock at markets or fairs. When someone bought a live piglet at a market, the merchant would place the animal in a sack so that the purchaser could get the goods home.

Problem was, sometimes those market merchants were less than upstanding. Instead of filling the sack with a valuable piglet, a merchant might try to pass off a useless cat. If (and really, when) that cat was let out of the bag, the merchant's secret was exposed. Of course, anyone who has tried to put a live cat in a bag knows that it's only a matter of seconds before that confined kitty will make a rather explosive exit. And doesn't that make sense? Secrets can be really hard to keep!

Sure, we can play dumb, lie, or politely refuse to tell. But in the end, we're all human, and we all seem to have this universal need to share our knowledge, experiences, and feelings with other people. (And sometimes, isn't it worth it just to see those stunned looks of shock and utter stupefaction?)

Daniel Wegner, a Harvard psychology professor who has studied the science behind secrets, says, "We don't realize that in keeping a secret, we've created an obsession in a jar." So try as you might to keep that cat in the bag, it's probably going to find its way out. Sorry, Aunt Miriam.

Q How come people have eyebrows?

A Quick. Draw a face. That's right—two eyes, a nose, and a mouth. You can turn the mouth up for a smile or down for a frown. But somehow your little face seems to lack expression. What's missing?

Add two short lines above the eyes. That's it! You can arch them up to convey surprise, even them out to indicate boredom, or pull them down into a V to show anger. With eyebrows, your face seems more alive—more, well, human.

Is this why we have eyebrows? To serve as a visual communication system? Actually, yes. According to anthropologists, one reason our highly mobile brows evolved was to give us the ability to signal each other when words just wouldn't do. When a predator was lurking nearby, for instance, or when teaching children who were too young for verbal communication. Cave mama's angry V said, "Keep away from the fire, kid!"

The other function of eyebrows is pretty obvious. Take a look at our ancestor Cro-Magnon man: His big, bushy protruding unibrow protected his eyes from falling leaves, volcanic ash, prehistoric flying insects, and other threats to his vision. Brows also collected sweat when he was out hunting mastodons. Brows still function as a runoff system for our sweat. The hairs point outward, to the sides of our face, to guide the droplets away from our eyes. If you have very thin brows or sweat a lot, you know how painful that burning sweat-in-the-eyes sensation can be. That's why dorky headbands evolved as an artificial unibrow.

Do other animals have eyebrows? Many mammals, including dogs and cats, have slight projections on the ridges above the eye sockets. Only primates—especially apes, which are considered to be our nearest evolutionary "cousins"—have recognizable brows. And yes, they use brows to communicate the same way we do. Primate ethologists—those who study the social lives of primates—know that an ape's raised brows can indicate anticipation: "Is that a banana you're holding?" The V can mean, "Better not try taking it away from me." And a quizzical furrow says, "Just kidding, right?"

Why do women have smaller brows than men? One theory is that women need more expressive faces because they do most of the child-rearing. Dainty brows have always been considered feminine. Back in the ultra-ladylike 1950s, some fashion mavens almost plucked themselves clean.

Interestingly enough, as men have become more equally involved in raising children, the smoother look has become more popular for them, too. Compare the current crop of clean-browed male movie stars to yesteryear's beetle-browed cowboys and you'll see what we mean.

Will eyebrows ever disappear entirely? Don't count on it. We'll always work up a sweat somehow, and we'll always need to communicate without using words. After all, what's an e-mail without an eyebrowed, winking emoticon that tells us, "Just kidding, right?"

Q How much beef jerky can you get out of a cow?

A There's a common misconception that men would starve to death if they were left to their own devices. This is patently untrue—as long as there's a convenience store nearby that sells beef jerky. Indeed, a beer, a baseball game, and a bag of beef jerky might make for the perfect afternoon for the average male. A serious beef jerky habit can get pretty expensive, though—even the cheap-o gas-station variety costs a few dollars for just a couple of ounces of dried, peppery goodness. It makes you wonder whether it wouldn't be easier just to cut out the middleman and go straight to the cattle auction.

As it turns out, you can get quite a bit of beef jerky from a single cow, but determining just how much requires a little agricultural mathematics. A large "beef animal" can weigh over twelve hundred pounds—this counts everything, including the guts, bones, and other inedible material. Before being turned into jerky, the cow needs to be butchered and trimmed into lean cuts (the best jerky is made from boneless steaks and roasts).

According to the agricultural school at South Dakota State University, the yield of an average cow that's butchered for lean beef is about 38 percent of its original weight—which means that a twelve hundred pound feeder will give you about 456 pounds of steaks, roasts, and ground beef with which to work. Next, the high-quality meat is cured and seasoned before being sliced into strips and dried. Meanwhile, the ground beef can be made into lower-quality jerky, which is labeled as "ground and formed" on the packaging. During the drying process, the meat loses up to three-quarters of its original weight; however, this still leaves us with a very generous portion of beef jerky from a single cow: roughly 115 pounds. Considering that an average bag of beef jerky weighs 1.8 ounces, we're talking more than a thousand bags of beef jerky from a single cow.

Of course, this is only a hypothetical situation—in the real world, the fattier cuts of meat are almost never used for jerky, because they're more difficult to dry and are (in their jerky form) much more perishable. Besides, as delicious as jerky is, steakhouse patrons know that there are other, more satisfying uses for the loin, tenderloin, and rib-eye cuts.

At any rate, when you consider the massive amount of work that's involved in butchering, cleaning, curing, slicing, and dehydrating a cow, it's probably better to leave it to the professionals. Hey, we've got baseball to watch.

Q How do you know if you're colorblind?

A Most people say, "Red means stop and green means go." But suppose you say, "The top light means stop and the bottom means go." Or maybe your friend offers to meet you in a crowded place, saying, "Just look for the guy in the yellow pants and the red and green polka-dot shirt." Instead of making fun of his taste, you reply, "You'd better wear a hat so I'll be sure to see you."

If the words "red" and "green" mean nothing to you, you probably have a condition known as deuteranomaly, or red-green color-blindness. It's the most common form of colorblindness and affects 5 to 8 percent of the world's male population. Other, rarer, forms of color blindness include the inability to distinguish blue from yellow (trichromacy) and total monochromacy, the inability to perceive any color.

Colorblindness may seem weird to people with normal vision, but actually, we've all been there. All human infants are born color-blind. We only begin to see color at around the age of four months when the retinas of our eyes are more developed.

How do we see color? The retina is composed of minute cells called rods and cones. The rods are most active in the dark, while the cones are most active in daylight. Because colors are most apparent in light, the cones are the main color receptors. We have three kinds of cones, and each absorbs one of three wavelengths of light: red, green, or blue. Scientists refer to this as trichromatic vision. The whole Crayola-box palette of colors our brains process comes from combining shades of red, yellow, and blue. It stands to reason, then, that any defect in one or more of the cones would affect our sense of color.

Colorblindness is considered a hereditary disorder. This is why fewer women are colorblind. A man, who has X and Y chromo-somes, only needs to inherit a gene for color blindness from one parent, while a woman, with her pair of X chromosomes, needs to inherit the gene from both parents.

How do you know if you are colorblind? The most common detector is the Ishihara Test, which consists of a series of colored numbers written in small dots against a contrasting background of similar dots. If you have trouble reading one or more of the numbers, you may have impaired color perception.

In most cases, colorblindness is not a serious disability. In fact, if you are colorblind, you're in good company. Fred Rogers—yes, *the* Mister Rogers—was colorblind. And Emerson Moser, a senior production worker at Crayola for thirty-seven years, was also colorblind. His co-workers didn't know until he told them upon his retirement in 1990. And your friend in the yellow pants and red and green polka-dot shirt? Hmmm. Come to think of it, he might be just a bit colorblind, too.

Q How come Pilgrims wore buckles on their hats?

A Thanksgiving is a special time of year. Americans gather around the holiday table to eat, drink, and give thanks. We're grateful for our health, our families, the bounty we're about to receive, and, most of all, for the evolution of fashion.

Why are we thankful fashion has evolved? Because we associate Thanksgiving with Pilgrims, and in the popular mind, Pilgrims dressed like deranged leprechauns: black pants, white collars, conical hats, buckles, buckles, and more buckles. Buckles on the shoes make a certain amount of sense. Buckles on the belt are understandable. But why in the world did Pilgrims need buckles on their hats?

Actually, Pilgrims didn't wear buckles on their hats—or anywhere else, for that matter. Most Pilgrims didn't wear black and white on a regular basis, either. The misconception that Pilgrims dressed dourly and had a buckle fetish is rooted in a long and proud tradition of Americans misunderstanding and misinterpreting their past.

It's time for a quick refresher on colonial history. The New England colonies were settled by two distinct groups of British colonists: the Pilgrims and the Puritans. Both the Pilgrims and the Puritans came to the New World because of religion, but they were decidedly different types of people.

The Pilgrims, led by William Bradford, came first, arriving on the *Mayflower* in Plymouth in 1620. They left England in search of religious freedom. The Pilgrims were separatists who wanted to break completely from the Anglican Church. These were the people who celebrated the first Thanksgiving.

The Puritans didn't arrive until 1630. They settled in Salem and founded the city of Boston. The Puritans were high-minded Anglicans who believed that the Anglican Church as it stood in England was corrupt and sinful. They came to the New World seeking to establish a "City on a Hill," a religious settlement. The Puritans never intended to break with the Anglican Church—they merely wanted to purify it.

Popular history has conflated the two groups, so when most Americans envision the early colonists, they imagine the drab black-and-white clothing the Puritans wore on special occasions. The Pilgrims rarely wore such clothing, preferring dyed violet, green, burgundy, brown, and other rich hues.

But what about the buckles? Neither group wore buckles on hats. Fashion historians date the popularity of buckles on hats (a short-lived trend) to the late seventeenth and early eighteenth centuries—a good eight decades after the Pilgrims celebrated the first Thanksgiving. Some historians suggest that the buckle motif found its way into portrayals of Pilgrims created during the late nineteenth century, when Thanksgiving became a national holiday and illustrators scrambled to depict the first Thanksgiving in popular media and children's books.

So next Thanksgiving, leave your buckled hat in the closet. But keep your belt buckle—you'll need something to loosen at the end of the meal.

Q How fast is a snail's pace?

A   The word "slow" hardly begins to cover it. These animals make all others look like Speedy Gonzales. Next to the snail, tortoises look like hares, and hares look like bolts of furry brown lightning.

Which brings to mind a bad joke: What did the snail riding on the tortoise's back say? *Whee!*

Garden snails have a top speed of about 0.03 mile per hour, according to *The World Almanac and Book of Facts*. However, snails observed in a championship race in London took the thirteen-inch course at a much slower rate—presumably because snails lack ambition when it comes to competition. To really get a snail moving, one would have to make the snail think its life was in jeopardy. Maybe the racing snails' owners should be hovering behind the starting line wearing feathered wings and pointed beaks, cawing instead of cheering.

The current record holder of the London race, the Guinness Gastropod Championship, is a snail named Archie, who made the trek in two minutes and twenty seconds in 1995. This calculates to 0.0053 mile per hour. At that rate, a snail might cover a yard in 6.4 minutes. If he kept going, he might make a mile in a little less than eight days.

In the time it takes you to watch a movie, your pet snail might travel about fifty-six feet. You could watch a complete trilogy, and your snail might not even make it out of the house. Put your pet snail on the ground and forget about him—he'll be right around where you left him when you get back.

So long as no one steps on him, that is.

Q How did Murphy get his own law?

A Murphy's Law holds that if anything can go wrong, it will. Not surprisingly, the most widely circulated story about the origin of Murphy's Law involves a guy named Murphy.

In 1949, Captain Edward A. Murphy, an engineer at Edwards Air Force Base in California, was working on Project M3981. The objective was to determine the level of sudden deceleration a pilot could withstand in the event of a crash. It involved sending a dummy or a human subject (possibly also a dummy) on a high-speed sled ride that came to a sudden stop and measuring the effects.

George E. Nichols, a civilian engineer with Northrop Aircraft, was the manager of the project. Nichols compiled a list of "laws" that presented themselves during the course of the team's work. For example, Nichols's Fourth Law is, "Avoid any action with an unacceptable outcome."

These sled runs were repeated at ever-increasing speeds, often with Dr. John Paul Stapp, an Air Force officer, in the passenger seat. After one otherwise-flawless run, Murphy discovered that one of his technicians had miswired the sled's transducer, so no data had been recorded. Cursing his subordinate, Murphy remarked, "If there is any way to do it wrong, he'll find it." Nichols added this little gem to his list, dubbing it Murphy's Law.

Not long after, Stapp endured a run that subjected him to forty Gs of force during deceleration without substantive injury. Prior to Project M3981, the established acceptable standard had been eighteen Gs, so the achievement merited a news conference. Asked how the project had maintained such an impeccable safety record, Stapp cited the team's belief in Murphy's Law and its efforts to circumvent it. The law, which had been revised to its current language before the news conference, was quoted in a variety of aerospace articles and advertisements, and gradually found its way into the lexicon of the military and of pop culture.

It's important to note that "laws" that are remarkably similar to Murphy's—buttered bread always lands face down; anything that can go wrong at sea will go wrong, sooner or later—had been in circulation for at least a hundred years prior to Project M3981. But even if Edward Murphy didn't break new ground when he cursed a technician in 1949, it's his "law" we quote when things go wrong, and that's all right.

Q How do those transparent teleprompters work?

A For those of you too busy watching Cartoon Network to be bothered with distractions like the State of the Union address, the technology in question is the seemingly transparent panes of glass flanking the president during a speech. Though this style of teleprompter has been used in other events, it has become so synonymous with speeches given by the president that it is colloquially known as a "presidential teleprompter." What kind of sorcery can deliver the content of a speech to a speaker without being seen by the audience?

While these teleprompters look like they're from the future, they are actually a modification of the type of system that is used in just about every TV newscast. With normal teleprompters, a monitor is placed perpendicular to the lens of a camera that displays the text the anchor reads. Then a half-silvered mirror—a piece of glass or plastic with a very thin reflective layer on one side, similar to the one-way mirror you'd find in an interrogation room—is placed at an angle in front of the camera lens and above the monitor. The mirror reflects the words on the monitor to the speaker but is transparent to the camera. The result is the illusion that the newscaster is staring directly into the camera, delivering line after line of flawless copy, apparently from memory.

The presidential teleprompter is a slight modification of this method. For this setup, two flat-screen LCD monitors are placed on the podium; they reflect the text upward onto two treated squares of glass that are like the aforementioned half-silvered mirror.

The next time you see a speech in which a presidential tele-prompter is used, notice how the glass is tilted toward the podium to catch the monitor's reflections instead of away from the speaker—it's the opposite of how a music stand, for instance, would be positioned to hold a sheet of paper. The result is that the glass panels appear blank to the audience while the speaker sees the reflected text from the LCD monitors. The glass is placed on both sides of the president so that our fearless leader won't miss a beat while "naturally" turning left and right to address both sides of the room.

So it's not magic at all, just boring old science. Sorry. Now you know why magicians never reveal the secrets behind their tricks.

Q How did people wake up before there were alarm clocks?

A Everyone has a trick for waking up on time. Some people put the alarm clock across the room so that they have to get out of bed to turn it off; some set the clock ahead by ten or fifteen minutes to try to fool themselves into thinking that it's later than it is; some set multiple alarms; and some—those boring Goody Two-Shoes types—simply go to bed at a reasonable hour and get enough sleep.

We don't necessarily rely on it every day, and some of us definitely don't obey it very often, but just about everybody has an alarm clock. How did people ever wake up before these modern marvels existed?

Many of the tough problems in life have a common solution: hire someone else to do it. Long ago in England, you could hire a guy to come by each morning and, using a long pole, knock on your bedroom window to wake you up so that you would get to work on time. This practice began during the Industrial Revolution of the late eighteenth century, when getting to work on time was a new and innovative idea. (In the grand tradition of British terminology that makes Americans snicker, the pole operator was known as a "knocker-up.") There's no word on how said pole operator managed to get himself up on time, but we can guess.

The truth is, you don't need any type of alarm, and you never did. Or so science tells us. Your body's circadian rhythms give you a sort of natural wake-up call via your body temperature's daily fluctuation. It rises every morning regardless of when you went to bed. Studies conducted at Harvard University seem to indicate that this rising temperature wakes us up (if the alarm hasn't already gone off).

Another study, conducted at the University of Lubeck in Germany, found that people have an innate ability to wake themselves up very early if they anticipate it beforehand. One night, the researchers told fifteen subjects that they would be awakened at 6:00 AM.

Around 4:30 AM, the researchers noticed that the subjects began to experience a rise in the stress hormone adrenocorticotropin. On the other two nights, the subjects were told that they would get a 9:00 AM wake-up call—but those diligent scientists shook them out of bed three hours early, at 6:00 AM. And this time, the adrenocorticotropin levels of the subjects held steady in the early morning hours.

It seems, then, that humans relied on their bodies to rouse them from the dream world long before a knocker-up or an alarm clock ever existed.

Q How do cats always find their way home?

A You can count on two things from your local television news during sweeps week: a story about a household appliance that is a death trap and another about a cat that was lost but somehow trekked thirty miles through a forest, across a river, and over an eight-lane highway to find its way home. You think, "No, I don't think my electric mixer is going to give me cancer, but, oh, that cat..."

What's the deal with felines? How do they always seem to be able to make it home, regardless of how far away home might be? No one knows for sure, but researchers have their theories. One study speculates that cats use the position of the sun as a navigational aid. Another posits that cats have a sort of built-in compass; this is based on magnetic particles that scientists have discovered on the "wrists" of their paws. While these are merely hypotheses, scientists know that cats have an advanced ability to store mental maps of their environments.

Exhibit A is Sooty, one of the felines chronicled on the PBS program *Extraordinary Cats*. Sooty traveled more than a hundred miles in England to return to his original home after his family moved. Sooty's feat, however, was nothing compared to that of Ninja, another cat featured on the program. A year after disappearing following his family's move, Ninja showed up at his old house, 850 miles away in a different state; he went from Utah back to Washington.

But there are limits to what a cat can do—that's why odysseys of felines like Sooty and Ninja are extraordinary. In other words, the odds aren't good that Snowball will reach your loving arms in Boston if you leave her in Pittsburgh.

Q How long can you live without sleep?

A Nobody knows for certain, but Dr. Nathaniel Kleitman, the father of modern sleep research, said: "No one ever died of insomnia." Still, what doesn't kill you can have some nasty side effects.

Various studies have revealed that missing just one night of sleep can lead to memory loss and decreased activity in certain parts of the brain. So if you're planning an all-night cram session for the evening before the big midterm, you may be better off closing the book and getting a good night's sleep.

Then again, maybe not. Each person's body and brain handle sleep deprivation differently. Some folks are all but useless after one night without shut-eye, while others function normally. It's largely a matter of physiology.

Take Tony Wright. In May 2007, the forty-three-year-old British gardener kept himself awake for 226 hours. He said that he was aiming for the world's sleeplessness record and wanted to prove that sleep deprivation does not diminish a person's coherence. Wright admitted to some odd sensory effects during his marathon, but he insisted that his mental faculties were not compromised.

Wright's quest didn't amount to much more than a lot of lost sleep. *Guinness World Records* stopped acknowledging feats of insomnia in 1990 after consulting with experts at the British Association for Counseling and Psychotherapy. The experts believe that sleep deprivation threatens psychological and physical well-being. Muscle spasms, reduced reaction times, loss of motivation, hallucinations, and paranoia can all be triggered by sleep deprivation. That Wright apparently didn't suffer any of these ill effects doesn't mean you won't. Sometimes, it seems, you lose if you don't snooze.

Q How come you never see famous people on jury duty?

A When people are summoned for jury duty, they are actually being summoned for a jury-selection process. If a case requires twelve people on the jury (most states use twelve jurors for trials, but some use six, especially in civil cases), the court may call in eighty people as potential jurors. The group then gets pared to eighteen (including six alternates).

If you think of jury duty as having to go to the courthouse for a day to take part in that selection process, celebrities do have to participate. Robert De Niro, Brad Pitt, Mariah Carey, Jerry Seinfeld, Uma Thurman, and scores of other celebs have been called to jury duty. Whether they end up serving on a jury is a different matter altogether.

For starters, anyone can stall a jury-duty summons for quite some time before running out of excuses. A simple phone call can get you a six-month respite, no questions asked. After that, there has to be a pretty good reason why you can't perform this civic duty.

At the jury selection, celebrities often argue their ways out of serving. Woody Allen sent a letter saying that he'd had a traumatic experience in court during a child-custody case with Mia Farrow and couldn't bear being in a courtroom again. The authorities didn't buy it, and he was ordered to show up. He arrived with his lawyer, his agent, and his bodyguard and refused to sit with other potential jurors, opting instead to stand. Eventually, he was allowed to leave. If acting like an arrogant celebrity doesn't work, there's always the chance that either side's attorney will dismiss the celebrity if the attorney thinks that the celebrity will influence the trial.

Sometimes celebrities are selected for a jury, though. In 2004 Oprah Winfrey served for a murder trial, and Rudolph Giuliani served for a minor trial in 1999 while he was mayor of New York. The trial involved a man who claimed that scalding hot shower water from an improperly maintained water heater burned his genitals, causing him to become impotent. The jury ruled against him.

Q How is it that in-laws are the butt of so many jokes?

A Feel beleaguered after a visit with the in-laws? Your situation is hardly unique. The phenomenon spans cultures, generations, and even millennia. Nearly two thousand years ago, the Roman poet Juvenal quipped, "Give up all hope of peace so long as your mother-in-law is alive."

Even then, the mother-in-law joke was told from the son-in-law's perspective. But the real victims of internecine in-law relations are daughters-in-law. Dr. Terri Apter, stressed-out daughter-in-law and Cambridge University psychologist, conducted a twenty-year study of the familial interactions of forty-nine couples and a large number of other people. More than 60 percent of the women reported strained relationships with their female in-laws. On the other hand, only about 15 percent of mother-in-law/son-in-law relationships generated dissatisfaction.

About two-thirds of the daughters-in-law Apter studied claimed that their mothers-in-law were jealous of them. Not surprisingly, roughly the same proportion of mothers-in-law complained of being excluded by their sons' wives. Why are in-law divisions especially prevalent among women?

Apter points to a couple of sources of tension: First, a mother-son relationship is a special bond, and the mother often feels her role being usurped when a new woman enters the picture. Then there's the daughter-in-law's struggle to establish competence in areas that often define women within families—childcare, cooking, maintenance of the home—and trying to do so in the shadow of her more experienced mother-in-law.

Men, Apter says, are often oblivious to the power struggle raging around them. Even if they recognize it, they're adept at feigning ignorance or laughing it off rather than addressing the problem. Maybe it's no coincidence that the name of that smart-aleck Roman poet was Juvenal rather than, say, Mature.

Q How did the term "bootleg" come to be associated with illegal activity?

A Coined in the seventeenth century, the term "bootleg" referred to, appropriately enough, the upper part of a boot. But thanks to good old American ingenuity, its meaning subsequently widened.

Bootlegs were handy for concealing all manner of things that a boot-wearer shouldn't have been carrying, from an extra gun to a bowie knife. In the late eighteen hundreds, bootlegs became effective storage places for illicit liquor that was subsequently traded to Native Americans.

The association between the word "bootleg" and the concealment of illegal alcohol was solidified with the onset of prohibition in the United States in 1920. Ships and trucks—which brought foreign-made liquor into the country from Canada, Mexico, the Bahamas, and Cuba—replaced bootlegs, but the intent was exactly the same, so the name stuck.

As the United States government refined its methods of locating contraband alcohol, the crafty smugglers adjusted, organizing into gangs and directing multifaceted enterprises. In addition to transporting booze, these growing syndicates produced and stored it. "Bootlegging" came to refer to every aspect of the smuggling process.

Prohibition laws were repealed in 1933, but the term "bootleg" has lived on. It is now used to describe any number of nefarious activities. For example, bootlegged booze has given way to bootlegged music. The parallel works just fine, but there is one problem: It's nigh on impossible to hide an illegally downloaded song in a bootleg.

Q How did the days of the week get their names?

A Just like our language itself, the English words for the days of the week embody a hodgepodge of influences. Some of them came from the ancient Babylonians and some came from the Romans. The rest were coined by the Anglo-Saxons, and you have our permission to blame these Germanic settlers of fifth-century Britain for all of the times that you misspelled "Wednesday" when you were a kid.

When the Babylonians established the seven-day week, they named the first day after the sun and the second after the moon.

Enter the Romans, who retained the names of those first two days as well as the Babylonians' custom of naming days for heavenly bodies and their representative deities. The Romans named the third day of the week for Mars, which was named after the god of war; the fourth for Mercury, god of merchants and messenger of the gods; the fifth for Jupiter, god of the sky, who brought rain and lightning; the sixth for Venus, goddess of love; and the last day of the week for Saturn, god of seed. The Romans then took along their calendar on a four-hundred-year visit to England. And when the Romans finally skedaddled back to Italy, in barged the Anglo-Saxons.

The Anglo-Saxons were so occupied with pillaging that they found time to rename only four of the seven days—they retained the sun, moon, and Saturn monikers. For the rest, the Anglo-Saxons—like those before them—turned to their gods. Interestingly, the Anglo-Saxons endeavored to identify each of their gods with its Roman predecessor.

So for the third day of the week, the Anglo-Saxons turned to Tiw, their god of war. For the fourth day, they chose Woden, the supreme deity. The fifth day went to Thor, god of thunder. And the sixth was named for their god of love, Frigg. (Yes, we're serious—Frigg.)

Variant spellings exist, but, basically, what the Anglo-Saxons called *sunnan daeg* is now Sunday. *Monan daeg* is now Monday. *Tiwes daeg* evolved into Tuesday. *Wodnes daeg* (which didn't evolve enough) became Wednesday. *Thorsdagr* is Thursday.

Frigedaeg is Friday. And *Saeterdag* is Saturday. And you now also have our permission to declare, "Thank Frigg it's Friday!"

Q How come a hockey puck is so hard to follow?

A If you have trouble following a hockey puck as it darts all over the ice, you're probably relatively new to the sport. Spectators who are indoctrinated enough to have lost a tooth or two in the stands—or at their local watering holes—during heated arguments about their favorite hockey teams have little trouble tracking that black blur, mostly because they can anticipate the action.

Hockey bills itself as the fastest sport around, and not just because of the puck. True, in the National Hockey League (NHL), a great scorer's slap shot can easily top one hundred miles per hour—in the 1960s, Chicago Blackhawks star Bobby Hull had a slapshot clocked at 120 miles per hour and a wrist shot at 105 miles per hour.

The players themselves are a blur, too. They skate at thirty miles per hour in sprinting situations and at twenty miles per hour when they're cruising down the ice. Such speed is rarely seen in the "foot" team sports, such as football, basketball, and baseball. So the frenetic action around the puck is part of what makes that black disc so hard to follow.

Still, the puck isn't completely innocent in this. At one inch thick and three inches in diameter, it's much smaller than a football or basketball. Hockey fans learn to keep tabs on the puck as they pick up on the nuances of the sport. They anticipate charges down the ice and take notice of how players position themselves for scoring opportunities, and they grow to appreciate the "nonpuck" plays, like checking and boxing out.

Watching hockey on television can be a challenge, and the Fox network tried to help with its use of the "smart puck" in the mid-1990s. Fox used the wonders of modern technology to transform the puck into a colored dot that had an easy-to-follow trail. The smart puck was widely panned for its distracting effect on the games. In fact, the only thing smart about it was that it went into cold storage after Fox's TV contract with the NHL expired. But the smart puck did have some value: It taught us that sometimes harder is better.

Q How come chefs wear such silly headgear?

A As anybody who has ever worked in a restaurant can attest, the chef is the supreme dictator of the kitchen. Sometimes brilliant, often tempestuous, the chef rules the back of the house through a combination of respect and fear. Still, how can someone wearing such a ridiculous hat be taken seriously?

Chefs may have the silliest headgear in the professional world. It's called a "toque blanche," and it is a white, heavily starched embarrassment whose look ranges from a tall tube to an enormous, deformed mushroom.

Just how it came to be the symbol of chefdom is a matter of debate. Indeed, there are several theories about the origin of the chef's toque, none of which is substantiated with enough evidence to be confirmed as a sole explanation. One of these is that Henry VIII, outraged at finding a hair in his soup, ordered the beheading of his chef. Future chefs took note, making sure to cover their heads in order to save them.

A second theory holds that the chef's toque originated in ancient Assyria, long before the birth of Christ. Back then, poisoning was the favored method of assassination (hence, the dangerous profession of the royal food taster). Obviously, a chef was under scrutiny because he had the power to poison food. Proof of the chef's allegiance to his royal master was a "crown" he fashioned—a tall hat, made of cloth, that mimicked the actual crown worn by the king himself.

A third theory, and perhaps the most compelling, is that the toque originated in the sixth century AD, in the beginning of the Middle Ages. In those dark days, artists and intellectuals—groups that included chefs—were persecuted, and it was said that some of these luminaries protected themselves by taking shelter in monasteries. To disguise themselves, they donned the wardrobe of the clergy, which apparently included silly hats.

Though the earliest origins of the toque are debatable, it is known that the headwear evolved into its current form in France, the birthplace of "haute cuisine." By the nineteenth century, forms of the toque were worn all over Europe, though their shapes varied.

In the late nineteenth century, the legendary French chef Auguste Escoffier brought order to the chaos and came up with a standard toque. Unfortunately, he decided that the tall, starched version of the chef's hat was ideal. In a way, it's not entirely surprising that the toque would find its ultimate form in France. It is the country, after all, that gave us another of the all-time silliest hats: the beret.

Q How can you identify a poisonous mushroom?

A Every gourmet knows that mushrooms can be among nature's delicacies—grilled portobello, stir-fried shiitake, and sautéed chanterelle mushrooms are mouthwatering treats. But what about the Destroying Angel, Weeping Fairy Cake, and Death Cap? As you can deduce from their names, these fungi don't belong anywhere near your lips.

How can you tell the good guys from the bad guys? There's no foolproof method—in fact, some of the most dangerous varieties are nearly indistinguishable from their edible cousins. The poisonous jack-o'-lantern mushroom, with its brightly colored cap, is easily mistaken for a yellow chanterelle. The delicious curly morel, characterized by a "brain-shaped" whorl, has an evil twin in the false morel, which also sports a spiraled top. Some of the most deadly mushrooms, the brown-capped *Galerina*, look as innocent as the varieties you'll find on your grocer's shelves.

Contrary to folk wisdom, boiling poisonous mushrooms will not neutralize their toxins. And don't assume that a fungus is safe just because you see a squirrel taking a nibble; animals can sometimes digest substances that would be fatal to human beings. Then what signs can you rely on? Naturalists suggest that you avoid any red-topped mushrooms with white dots. They may look like the cute toadstools in children's storybooks, but the fly agaric contains a powerful hallucinogenic substance, muscimol, that can send you on a really bad trip. If you see a ring high on a mushroom's stem and a cup where the stem meets the ground, chances are you've found an *Amanita phalloides*—the infamous Death Cap.

The umbrella-shaped, green-spored *Lepiota* also have rings around their stems. *Lepiota* often cluster in "fairy rings" in meadows or on lawns. Though they're not lethal, they can give you a serious case of gastric distress. Above all, keep away from LBMs, or Little Brown Mushrooms. Ranging in color from pale tan to dark chestnut, most are harmless, but you never know if a deadly *Galerina* lurks among them.

If you want to go mushroom hunting, invest in a field guide, such as one published by the Audubon Society. Remember, however, that mushrooms in the wild are rarely picture-perfect—age and the damage caused by weather, insects, and animals can alter a mushroom's appearance and eradicate many of the telltale signs of danger.

The best advice is to never eat a mushroom that seems the least bit suspect. If you exercise an extra measure of caution and common sense, you'll find that you can have your favorite fungi and eat them, too.

Q How did high school proms get started?

A The word itself seems to have come from slang-happy college students of the late eighteen hundreds and early nineteen hundreds. It was originally a shortened form of "promenade," meaning the entry and announcement of guests at a formal dance, and then it became a term for college dances in general. The earliest known reference to a prom can be found in an Amherst College student's 1894 journal entry; it likely referred to a senior class dance held at nearby Smith College.

But what about high school dances—proms, specifically? They are more closely related to upper-class debutante balls than to college dances. The debutante ball originated in sixteenth-century England as a formal way to present a young woman who was available for marriage. The tradition spread to America in the late nineteenth century and flourished among the wealthy as a rite of passage to adulthood. In the early twentieth century, middle-class parents wanted the opportunity to give their own kids similar tastes of adulthood, so they began organizing high school dances. References to these proms started popping up in high school yearbooks in the 1930s, but some communities were likely holding these events earlier than that.

Early proms were far cries from the extravaganzas of today. High school kids would dress up in their Sunday best, go to the school gym, enjoy some refreshments, and cut a rug—all under the watchful eyes of adults. Limousines and tuxedos weren't yet part of the equation.

As America's middle class grew more prosperous in the 1950s, kids and parents spent more money on proms. In turn, the importance of these dances increased. Some schools moved them out of their gyms and into hotel ballrooms; young men started cramming themselves into formal wear, and young ladies began dropping loads of cash on special prom dresses. The popularity of proms waned a bit in the 1960s, when everybody who was anybody rebelled against everything. But proms came back strong in the mid-1980s, fueled by a popular string of romantic teen comedies, such as *Footloose* and *Pretty in Pink*.

These days, proms are big business. Some estimates place total annual U.S. prom expenditures at more than two billion dollars. In 2007, *Seventeen* magazine estimated that the girl alone drops an average of eight hundred dollars on her senior prom. That's a lot of money to spend for a date with a guy you'll probably never see again after graduation.

Q How does yeast make dough rise?

A Croissant. Brioche. San Francisco sourdough. If not for the modest, single-celled fungus known as yeast, we would be condemned to a life of lavash (a.k.a. flat, airless cracker bread).

Yeast can turn a glob of dough into a beautifully risen baguette, and the process is really quite simple. Yeast is a living microscopic organism that doesn't require much to work its magic—just moisture (water), food (sugar or starch), and a warm (seventy to eighty-five degrees Fahrenheit), nurturing environment. When mixed with water and flour to make bread, yeast is truly in a happy place. It feeds on the starchy nutrients that are found in the flour and, through the process of fermentation, converts these nutrients into ethanol and carbon dioxide gas.

This carbon dioxide moves into air bubbles within the bread dough. If the dough is a strong, elastic ball of gluten mesh (like it ought to be), the gas will get trapped within these air bubbles and inflate them. As more and more of these tiny air bubbles fill up, the dough begins to rise and expand.

Once the bread is in the oven, heat kills the yeast and burns off the alcohol. And while yeast is mostly known as a leavening agent, it also contributes to bread's flavor.

 How old does an item have to be to be considered an antique?

A Depends on whom you ask. Bet you knew we were going to say that.

The United States Customs Service classifies items that are at least one hundred years old as genuine antiques, at least for import purposes. Items of that age can be brought into the country duty-free.

Some old-school purists claim that the term "antique" can only apply to things made before 1820. By that time, the Industrial Revolution was in full swing, and that year marks a point at which handcrafted items were being widely replaced by machine-made goods.

The word itself is closely related to the word "antiquities." At one point, "antiquities" meant "treasures from ancient times"—think Rome, Greece, Egypt, and Mesopotamia. Later on, the word "antique" took on different shades of meaning, conjuring images of the handmade items of a bygone age, lusted after and collected by people who don't value factory-made stuff.

No doubt nostalgia has increased the prices of those pre-1820 handcrafted tables and plates, just as nostalgia plays a role today when we price and trade collectibles. Is Depression glass antique? How about Bakelite trinkets, or Howdy Doody lunch-boxes? By the definitions above, no, they are not antiques.

Vintage, collectible, or antique: If collectors are willing to pay thousands of dollars for these objects, does it really matter what they are called?

Q How do we know that elephants never forget?

A Elephants would be excellent in the business world. Working elephants in Myanmar have been shown to remember verbal commands, other animals, and people. Considering the way they store memories of their interactions, elephants appear biologically disposed to networking. An elephant never draws a blank, leading to the famous saying: "An elephant never forgets."

Studies have revealed that as an elephant ages, its memory improves. When approached by an outsider, a matriarch often signals to the rest of the herd whether the stranger is a friend or a foe. She uses her personal experiences, as well as her sense of smell and contact cues, to protect her brood from rogue and possibly violent bull elephants. The matriarch passes her knowledge on to other members of her herd. (This was determined from a study of twenty-one elephant families during a seven-year period in Kenya.)

The same survival instinct comes into play when an elephant smells a member of a familiar group that is known to kill elephants. When an elephant catches a whiff of one of these hunters, it will race for safety. If the elephant smells a member of a group that is known to not kill elephants, it will continue grazing in the area. The elephant remembers scents, and it can differentiate between one that means danger and one that doesn't.

The saying itself is likely an alteration of an old Greek proverb: "A camel never forgets an injury." Camels were swapped out for elephants early in the twentieth century, after intelligence and an impressive capacity for recall were observed in the latter. It has become common to say someone has an "elephantine" memory—which is much more acceptable than saying that someone has an elephantine body.

Q How close are we to teleporting, like they do in *Star Trek*?

A Closer than you think, but don't squander those frequent-flyer miles just yet. There's a reason why Captain Kirk is on TV late at night shilling for a cheap-airfare Web site and not hawking BeamMeToHawaiiScotty.com. For the foreseeable future, jet travel is still the way to go.

If, however, you're a photon and need to travel a few feet in a big hurry, teleportation is a viable option.

Photons are subatomic particles that make up beams of light. In 2002, physicists at the Australian National University were able to disassemble a beam of laser light at the subatomic level and make it reappear about three feet away. There have been advances since, including an experiment in which Austrian researchers teleported a beam of light across the Danube River in Vienna via a fiber-optic cable—the first instance of teleportation taking place outside of a laboratory.

These experiments are a far cry from dematerializing on your spaceship and materializing on the surface of a strange planet to make out with an alien who, despite her blue skin, is still pretty hot. But this research demonstrates that it is possible to transport matter in a way that bypasses space—just don't expect teleportation of significant amounts of matter to happen until scientists clear a long list of hurdles, which will take many years.

Teleportation essentially scans and dematerializes an object, turning its subatomic particles into data. The data is transferred to another location and used to recreate the object. This is not unlike the way your computer downloads a file from another computer miles away. But your body consists of trillions upon trillions of atoms, and no computer today could be relied on to crunch numbers powerfully enough to transport and precisely recreate you elsewhere.

As is the case with many technological advances, the most vexing and long-lasting obstacle probably won't involve creation of the technology, but rather the moral and ethical issues surrounding its use. Teleportation destroys an object and recreates a facsimile somewhere else. If that object is a person, does the destruction constitute murder? And if you believe that a person has a soul, is teleportation capable of recreating a person's soul within the physical body it recreates? And should we someday cross that final frontier, if BeamMeToHawaiiScotty.com becomes a reality, do you believe that William Shatner should star in the television commercial?

Q How do I become a human guinea pig?

A Ever want to do something for the good of all humankind? How about jogging on a treadmill with an oxygen mask strapped to your face? (Whew!) Or sleeping with a dozen electrodes attached to your body and a video camera watching? (Yikes!) Or eating a diet of specially prepared vegetarian food for three months? (Yum!) Or sniffing cotton balls saturated with the sweat of strangers of the opposite sex? (Phew!)

All of these are ways in which people have participated in clinical trials. Clinical trials have given doctors insight into how we breathe, dream, absorb nutrients, and even sniff out our soul mates. Thousands of these trials take place every year. How can you become a volunteer? The government maintains a comprehensive database of these trials at ClinicalTrials.gov, which will point you in the right direction. And if you live near a teaching hospital, you can call and ask if it has a department of clinical research.

Before you hand yourself over to eager medical students, however, you should know that in order to qualify as a genuine clinical trial, the experiment must have a set of rules, or protocols. Protocols define every step of a trial, including how volunteers are chosen, what kinds of treatment they receive, and how the results are measured.

If you qualify, you will be asked to sign a document testifying that you have given your informed consent. Don't take this lightly: You may very well be going where no man or woman has gone before. Though the vast majority of trials are safe, the effects of various medical treatments can't be guaranteed, even by the most careful researchers.

At the beginning of a study, volunteers are divided into several groups. One group, the control group, receives no treatment whatsoever. If the study involves medication, the control group will be given a placebo, which is usually a fake pill made of sugar and cellulose.

You've heard of the placebo effect? That's when the pseudo-pill-popping volunteers respond as if they are taking the real thing. It might be embarrassing to find out afterward that your amazing improvement was all in your mind, but the placebo effect is so important that a whole branch of clinical trials has evolved just to study it. Sort of like trials to test trials.

Will you be paid? Sometimes. Payment, if offered, depends upon the length and complexity of the trial. It may be as little as ten dollars for a test that only takes an hour, but you could make several hundred dollars for trials that require hospital stays.

For most people, volunteering for a clinical trial is a one-shot deal. However, a small number of intrepid individuals actually turn it into a full-time job. A career as a professional human guinea pig may not be everyone's cup of antioxidant green tea, but it sure can provide some interesting conversation at Thanksgiving when Aunt Edna leans over and says, "So tell me, dear, what do you do for a living?"

Q How did the Dear John letter get its name?

A Everyone knows that when a guy receives a Dear John letter, it means he's being dumped by his girlfriend. But who the heck is John?

The term originated in World War II, when thousands of American men were stationed overseas, far from their wives and girlfriends. These separations strained relationships to the limit, and usually, it was the girls back home who wanted out. "Dear," of course, was the typical way to start a letter; John was a common name at the time—it still is, though its popularity has waned in recent decades. But there's more to our answer than that.

The name John has a long history as an alias for an unknown or unidentified man, as in "John Doe" or "John Q. Public." It has also been assigned to generic soldiers in patriotic songs, including "When Johnny Comes Marching Home" from the Civil War and "Over There," which was popular during both World War I and World War II and includes the line "Johnnie, get your gun."

Furthermore, *Dear John* was a popular radio program that ran from 1933 to 1944. The main character was a female who often read letters that began with the words "Dear John" (although she wasn't breaking up with a boyfriend).

Dear John letters are still being sent, but they are more likely to be emails or text messages than pieces of paper that are sealed in envelopes. Of course, that doesn't make them any less painful.

Q How many countries have a neutralist policy?

A Bent on world domination? To an aspiring dictator, neutral countries can look like the low-hanging fruit on the tree of global conquest. They lack offensive military capabilities and they have wishy-washy foreign policies—in other words, they are there for the taking. Or so it would seem. In fact, this whole "neutral" thing is a lot more complicated than it looks.

First of all, there's a difference between being "neutral" and "neutralist." A neutralist country is one that has a policy of non-alignment: When it seems like the whole world is picking sides in an extended conflict, a neutralist country tries to stay out of it.

The neutralist movement dates to the Cold War, when some countries refused to affiliate with either the Soviet bloc or the Western bloc of nations. India is one of the largest countries that had a neutralist policy—it tried to (ahem) curry favor with the USSR and the USA alike. But a neutralist policy doesn't mean a country must avoid aggression. Neutralist countries have gone to war with each other, like Iran and Iraq did in the early 1980s.

So how many neutralist countries are there? A lot. So many that they have their own international organization, the Non-Aligned Movement (NAM), which represents most of the countries in South America, Africa, and the Middle East. And though the NAM has been called a relic of the Cold War, it's still alive and kicking.

Now, a "neutral" country is something else entirely. Neutrality is a condition that is recognized by the international laws and treaties that govern warfare. According to these agreements, when a war breaks out, disinterested countries can declare themselves neutral. This means that they have certain rights—the warring nations can't enter their territories, for example—as well as the fundamental responsibility to remain neutral by treating the warring nations impartially. Any country can potentially remain neutral during any war, as long as it can maintain that impartiality.

But this idea of limited neutrality doesn't really get to the heart of our question. We're looking for perpetually neutral countries—the Swedens and the Switzerlands of the world. Switzerland, as you may recall, has had guaranteed neutrality since the Congress of Vienna settled Napoleon's hash in 1815, and the Swedes have been neutral since about that time as well. But although Sweden stayed out of the great wars of the twentieth century, its current neutrality is debatable since it's a member of the European Union (EU) and, as such, has a stake in the EU's non-neutral foreign policy.

That leaves the Swiss. But before you start drawing up your marching orders against the soft underbelly of Switzerland, you should get familiar with the phrase "armed neutrality." This means that the Swiss aren't going to roll over for you—they've got a defensive army, or more accurately, a sort of citizen militia. Switzerland also has one of the highest gun-ownership rates in the world. So beware, aspiring dictators: This world-domination thing isn't as easy as it looks.

Q How is it that you're born with tonsils if they aren't necessary?

A We may not *need* tonsils, but they're pretty useful nonetheless. Tonsils are part of the lymphatic system, which is a major component of the all-important immune system. The immune system, of course, is what hunts down and destroys or disarms the various harmful viruses and bacteria that infect our body.

Tonsils are designed to trap germs that come in through your nose and mouth. They also produce antibodies and immune cells that break down and get rid of those sneaky germs. So you shouldn't be in any hurry to remove them.

However, like everything else in the human body, tonsils aren't completely invincible. They can get infected themselves, resulting in swelling, infection, and general painful, oozy unpleasantness. Beyond the pain, this swelling can cause breathing problems, especially in young children, whose tonsils are already quite large in relation to their throats.

Nowadays, doctors don't like to remove tonsils without plenty of justification. But if you do need to have your tonsils taken out, don't fret too much. Going under the knife usually won't lead to any adverse long-term effects, since tonsils are too small a part of the lymphatic system to make a massive difference in your overall health. Your body can manage without them; it's very well designed. Still, if your tonsils are not causing you any major problems, just hang on to them and let them do their germ-fighting thing. It can't hurt.

Q How come we have food cravings?

A Got a hankering for some steamed carrots and Brussels sprouts? Didn't think so. Most cravings are of the sweet, salty-crunchy, super-high-fat varieties. But just what is it that prompts us to make a mad dash to the 7-Eleven for Funyuns and Ding Dongs in the middle of the night?

Researchers aren't exactly sure, but one theory that's gaining acceptance speculates that food cravings are actually addictions. How so? Brain image studies conducted by Marcia Pelchat, a sensory psychologist at the Monell Chemical Senses Center in Philadelphia, show that food cravings activate parts of the brain that are typically involved with habit formation. Known as the caudate nucleus, this is the same region of the brain that's affected by cocaine, alcohol, and cigarettes. "Think of food cravings as a sensory memory," says Pelchat. "You remember how good it felt the last time you had that food."

It all has to do with a food's biological and emotional resonance. Brian Wansink, a food psychology expert and the author of *Mindless Eating: Why We Eat More Than We Think*, agrees that people crave foods that connect them to pleasant experiences.

Men, he says, are drawn toward hearty meals—such as barbecue ribs, burgers, meat loaf, pasta, pizza—because they associate those foods with a nurturing wife or mother. Women, on the other hand, connect those same savory meals to long hours spent in the kitchen. Wansink notes that chocolate and ice cream don't involve any prep work or cleanup, which may help to explain why women are drawn to those types of sweets. That's right, ladies—just flip the lid off that pint of Häagen-Dazs and you've got one quick euphoria fix.

But what about the "wisdom of the body" theory, which states that our bodies simply crave what we nutritionally need? Pelchat says that wisdom doesn't apply, unless you're a sodium-deficient rodent: "When rats are salt deprived, they show a sodium appetite; they seem to be able to detect amino acids when they're protein deprived. But there's actually very little evidence for that in people. A lot of people in our society crave salty foods, but very few are actually salt deficient."

So that sudden urge to hit the A&W drive-thru isn't exactly motivated by nutritional necessity. You're really just addicted to the chili cheese fries.

Q How do animals know when an earthquake is coming?

A One of the holy grails of scientific research is the ability to accurately predict earthquakes. The number of lives saved could be in the thousands per quake. It seems bizarre to think that animals are capable of something science has failed to accomplish, but evidence going back thousands of years suggests that animals know when an earthquake is coming. How do they do it?

We really have no idea. In fact, there is a great deal of debate as to whether animals actually have the ability to predict earthquakes, and few Western scientists consider the topic serious enough to research. Most of the evidence is anecdotal. No one has been able to duplicate predictive ability in a laboratory test, nor have any studies revealed what mechanism might allow for such predictive powers. The U.S. Geological Survey's official position on the matter is that "consistent and reliable behavior prior to seismic events, and a mechanism explaining how it could work, still eludes us."

There are many stories of animals acting strangely in the weeks, days, or hours preceding a quake. Examples include stampeding horses in Chile in 1835, snakes ending their hibernations early and leaving their holes in China in 1974, dogs and wolves howling incessantly in Italy in 1783, and the appearance of thousands of toads on a street in China in 2008. The stories involve a wide range of species and behaviors.

Skeptics suggest that the strange animal behavior is only linked to the earthquake event in hindsight, and that unusual behaviors occur all the time for any number of reasons (weather, hunger, the presence of other animals, etc.), but no one notices when an earthquake *doesn't* happen. Also, many of the reports come from places rather distant from the earthquake itself (the toads in China appeared three hundred fifty miles away from the quake's epicenter), making the connection tenuous at best.

Chinese authorities have devoted a great deal of effort to earthquake prediction using animals, and they have claimed success in many cases. In 1975 they evacuated the city of Haicheng, and a few days later a large earthquake struck. Although Chinese officials reported that animal behavior was used for the prediction, it was later revealed that a series of foreshocks (rare pre-quake tremors) had been the real clue.

Suppose that animals *can* predict earthquakes—what physiological mechanism would be at work? One theory suggests that the movement of rocks deep below the surface of the earth releases electric energy that affects the earth's magnetic field and can be detected by animals. Others think the presence of magnetite, a magnetic mineral found in some animals, is the answer. Some species rely on the planet's magnetic field to orient their migration patterns, so a random pattern of magnetic fluctuations released by subsurface changes could drive the animals absolutely haywire.

Ultimately, it may be true that animals sense earthquakes in some way, but this ability is probably not reliable or accurate enough to allow humans to make any serious, useful seismic predictions.

Q How do you become an icon?

A In the old days, not just anyone could become an icon. You couldn't merely be a successful CEO or a chart-topping guitar player—you pretty much had to be Jesus Christ. Or the Blessed Virgin Mary. Or a saint. And even if you attained such rarefied prominence, you weren't an icon—your image was an icon.

The term "icon" comes from the Greek word *eikon*, meaning "image" or "likeness." In Byzantine and other Eastern churches, depictions of religious figures, which were typically presented on wooden panels, were considered sacred and came to be known as icons.

In modern pop culture, an icon is anyone who's synonymous with a particular movement, idea, or group of individuals. Picture Ronald Reagan, and you think of 1980s conservatism; see Elvis, and you think of '50s rock and roll. Billionaire investor Carl Icahn might not be an icon per se, but headline writers seem to love the homophone (it's not what you think; look it up).

But how do you become an icon? Follow this simple two-step process: (1) be scrupulously true to your ideals, and (2) get really, really famous. That's all there is to it.

Q How much room do you need to swing a cat?

A Quarters are tight here in the Q&A war room. Towers of folders that are overflowing with archival research teeter dangerously over our postage-stamp-size desks, where we slave away amongst a heady blend of ink, paper, and each other. It's not pleasant. Anyway, in our cramped office, the following phrase is frequently muttered with dismay: "There's not enough room in here to swing a cat." And that got us wondering: Just how much room might one need to accomplish the task?

To answer this question, we need to trace the phrase's origin. There are multiple theories, and, no, they have nothing to do with the Jazz Age and all of its swingin' cats. Furthermore, according to the first explanation, the phrase might not even have anything to do with felines. It seems that back in the seventeenth and eighteenth centuries, any sailor in the British navy who misbehaved was rewarded with a flogging with a whip that featured nine knotted lashes. This menacing little device was known as a "cat o' nine tails." Because a great deal of open space was required for the whip to be used effectively—and because floggings were frequently done in view of other sailors as a lesson—the old cat o' nine tails was only broken out in a spacious area, such as the poop deck.

A second camp argues that the phrase originated with a medieval archery game in which a cat was put into a leather bag and swung from the nearest tree or rafter and used for target practice. This theory has some weaknesses, not the least of which is determining a conceivable reason for archers to practice so cruelly. There is also little historical evidence to back up this claim, though in Shakespeare's *Much Ado About Nothing*, the cantankerous Benedick says, "If I do, hang me in a bottle like a cat and shoot at me; and he that hits me, let him be clapped on the shoulder, and called Adam."

Neither of these theories seems to indicate that there was ever a time when people were swinging actual felines by the tail. But what if you wanted to? It seems clear that swinging a cat requires space, but just how much? Fortunately, we remember our geometry. Let's say that the average cat is about twenty-four inches long and that its tail is about twelve inches long. We also need space for our arms, and the average human male's arms are twenty-eight inches long.

This means we'll need sixty-four inches, or more than five feet of swinging radius. Recalling our handy little formula for the area of a circle, we know that the total area required is 12,867 inches. Of course, most rooms aren't circular. The area of a square room with sides of 128 inches (the diameter of our circle) is about 114 square feet.

In other words, a space far, far larger than our office.

Q How does glow-in-the-dark stuff work?

A Switch off the light in the bedroom of a typical eight-year-old and you might see a ceiling glowing with stars, planets, and dinosaurs. "'Tis vile witchcraft!" you may shout, reaching around for some rope and a torch. Wait! Before you burn the kid at the stake, let's review simple physics.

Atoms gain and lose energy through the movement of electrons. Electrons are the tiny, negatively charged particles that orbit the atom's positively charged nucleus. When something energizes an atom, an electron jumps from a lower orbital (closer to the atom's nucleus) to a higher orbital (farther from the atom's nucleus).

Basically, the atom is storing energy that will be released in some form when the electron falls back to the lower orbital.

Light is one thing that can energize an atom in this way. When a light photon (an individual packet of light energy) hits the atom, that energy boosts an electron to a higher orbital. Some atoms can release energy as light: When the electron falls back to a lower orbital, the stored extra energy is emitted as a light photon.

Glow-in-the-dark stuff contains atoms that do just this; they're called phosphors. When you turn on the lights in your kid's room, the photons from the light excite these atoms and boost their electrons to higher orbitals. When you turn off the lights, the atoms release the stored energy. The electrons return to a lower level, emit photons, and the atoms glow. There's some energy loss in the process, so the glowing light of the little dinosaur will be of a different frequency (a different color) than the light that excited the atom in the first place.

Phosphors are everywhere. Your fingernails, teeth, and bodily fluids all contain natural phosphors. Your white clothes are phosphorescent too, thanks to whitening agents in laundry detergent. This is why all this stuff glows under a black light. The black light emits invisible ultraviolet light, which causes the phosphors to glow. (Dark clothes may contain phosphors, too, but the dark pigments absorb the UV light.)

Most phosphors have very short persistence—the atoms release the light energy immediately after they're charged, so they glow only when light is shining on them. By contrast, glow-in-the-dark stickers and the like are made of phosphors such as zinc sulfide and strontium aluminate that have unusually long persistence, so they keep glowing after you turn out the lights. Manufacturers mix these phosphors with plastic to make glow-in-the dark items in many shapes and sizes.

Other types of phosphors react to radiation from radioactive elements and compounds rather than from visible light radiation. This is how the hands on some watches glow with no charging required: They're coated with a radioactive isotope of hydrogen called tritium or promethium that's mixed with phosphors.

As you now know, there's a scientific explanation for glowing stars on the bedroom ceiling. So you can put away the rope and the torch.

Q How come you can get a grade of A, B, C, D, or F on your term paper, but not an E?

A You actually can get a grade of E on a paper—it all depends on where you go to school. Most schools in the United States use the A-to-F grading system, with A being the best grade and F the worst, skipping E entirely. There are many variations of this system—such as pluses and minuses that are appended to the letter—that are more common in American universities.

In the E-G-S-U grading system, which is used by some graduate schools as well as some primary and elementary schools, E stands for "excellent," G for "good," S for "satisfactory," and U for "unsatisfactory." To further complicate the issue, pluses and minuses are sometimes used. Some schools use an N instead of a U for "not satisfactory."

If a school is using the A-to-F system, it doesn't include an E for a couple of reasons. If the E were used, getting one would be only slightly better than failing. Some schools in other countries use it this way. But those who are familiar with the E-G-S-U system might be confused by an E. Your parents might think that you got an "excellent" instead of nearly failing. It's also easy to change an F to an E with a tiny pen stroke. So to avoid both confusion and the possibility of grade falsification, there's no E in the A-to-F system. Before the nearly universal adoption of the A-to-F system, however, some schools did use an E for "failure." But once you start considering the different ranges of percentage points that would correspond to each letter grade, it gets pretty complicated.

It might be easier to go the route of some universities, such as Bennington College and Sarah Lawrence College, which use narrative evaluations instead of letter grades. (A student can request a letter-grade equivalent at Bennington.) However, that glowing narrative posted on the refrigerator door may not make as much of an impact as a term paper with a big letter A on it. There's no way to cheat, either.

Q How do cats purr?

A Devoted cat owners know that no sound is quite as pleasant as the purr of a happy cat. That deep, throaty rumble seems to be the essence of contentment. How do cats do it? Well, it's a purr-fect mystery.

The problem, of course, is that you can't see inside a purring cat. To get an idea of what's going on, scientists turned to electromyography, a process that uses electrodes to measure how and when nerves make muscles contract. Purring cats expand and contract the muscles around the larynx, or "voice box," which contains the vocal cords. This rapid muscle motion causes the air in the box to vibrate as it is pushed in and out of the glottis, a small, narrow space between the vocal cords. At least that's one theory. Cats aren't about to tell us how they do it.

Animal behaviorists do know a little more about *why* cats purr, though. Kittens initially learn to purr from their mothers on their second day of life. Because kittens are born blind and deaf, the vibrations of the momma cat's purr act as an all-safe signal, letting her kittens know she's home and ready to nurse them. You may have noticed your cat making kneading motions with its paws when it purrs. Kittens do this when they nurse because kneading promotes milk flow. By kneading, a kitten is saying, "I'm feeling safe and warm and good, just like I did when Momma was taking care of me." Cats can't purr with their mouths open, but they can purr while nursing. If your cat is kneading you, it may also mean, "I'm hungry. When's dinner?"

But cats don't purr only when they're happy. They've been known to purr when they're injured, in pain, and when they're stressed, perhaps to comfort themselves. Before you panic, however, be aware that the "pain" purr is usually deeper than a regular purr and is accompanied by other distress signs, such as sensitivity to touch, refusal to eat, and constant licking or scratching of an injured or irritated limb.

Why would an injured cat purr? Again, no one is quite sure, although there's a theory that cats may purr due to a release of endorphins. It may also be an instinctive way of calling for help quietly, without drawing the attention of creatures that might want to prey on an injured cat. If you think your cat is asking for your help, make him as comfortable as you can and then call a vet to find out what your next step should be.

Otherwise, if your cat is purring with his normal blissed-out expression, you can kick back, relax, and enjoy it. Just like him.

Q How crazy do you have to be to be considered legally insane?

A No, judges don't keep a "You must be *this* nuts to get out of jail" sign hidden behind their benches. But you can be found not guilty by reason of insanity if you're cuckoo in just the right way.

Criminal insanity doesn't refer to any specific mental disorder, but it is related to mental illness. The reasoning behind the insanity defense is that some mental disorders may cause people to lose the ability to understand their actions or to differentiate between right and wrong, leaving them unable to truly have criminal intent. Intent is an important element of crime. If you intentionally burn down a house by dropping a lit cigarette in a trash can, we'd call you an arsonist. But if you do exactly the same thing accidentally, we'd probably just call you an inconsiderate (and perhaps a criminally negligent) jerk.

Similarly, the reasoning goes, you shouldn't be punished if a mental illness leads you to break the law without really comprehending your actions. Now, this doesn't apply to just any run-of-the-mill murderer with an antisocial personality disorder. A lack of empathy may lead someone to commit crimes, but if he understands what he's doing and he realizes that what he's doing is wrong, he's not insane.

You can only be found not guilty by reason of insanity in two cases: if mental illness keeps you from understanding your actions and deprives you of the ability to tell right from wrong, or if mental illness leaves you unable to control your actions and you experience an irresistible impulse to commit a crime. Details vary from state to state (and some states don't recognize the insanity defense at all), but these are the general criteria.

Some form of the insanity defense seems to date back to the sixteenth century, but early versions were awfully hazy. The 1843 trial of Daniel M'Naghten helped to clear things up. Thinking that the pope and English Prime Minister Robert Peel were out to get him, M'Naghten went to 10 Downing Street to kill Peel but ended up killing Peel's secretary. Witnesses claimed that M'Naghten was delusional, and the jury found him not guilty by reason of insanity. Queen Victoria was none too pleased, so a panel of judges was convened to clarify the rules governing the insanity defense as it involved the inability to distinguish right from wrong.

The definition has been controversial ever since, and every high-profile case in which it is invoked seems to throw the idea into question. Patty Hearst and Jeffery Dahmer both tried to use the insanity defense unsuccessfully, while David Berkowitz (Son of Sam) and Ted Kaczynski (the Unabomber) seemed ready to pursue the defense but ultimately decided against it. But a jury did acquit John Hinckley Jr. of all charges related to his assassination attempt on President Reagan after it determined that he was insane.

A successful insanity plea is rare. In the 1990s, a study funded by the National Institute of Mental Health found that defendants pleaded insanity in less than 1 percent of cases, and that only a quarter of those pleas were successful. Those who are successful hardly ever get off scot-free—they're simply committed to mental institutions rather than sent to prisons. On average, those who are found insane end up spending more time confined to an institution than they would have in prison if they had been found guilty.

So unless you really love padded rooms, it's probably best to try another defense.

Q How did the cocktail get its name?

A In *The Spy*, James Fennimore Cooper's 1821 novel about the American Revolution, secret agents and double agents reconnoiter in a smoky tavern that's overseen by an Irish woman named Betty Flanagan. In addition to her loyalty and courage, "Betty," Cooper tells us, "had the merit of being the inventor of that beverage which is so well known at the present hour to all the patriots … and which is distinguished by the name of 'cocktail.'"

Did an Irish barmaid in Westchester County, New York, really concoct the first cocktail around 1780? According to one legend, the cocktail does indeed go back to the days of the American Revolution. Supposedly, Continental soldiers and their French allies liked to kick back at local inns after a hard day of fighting off British redcoats. The Americans usually opted for shots of whiskey or gin, while the suaver French preferred wine, sherry, or vermouth.

One evening, some soldiers decided that they wanted a little dinner—perhaps a bit of *coq au vin*—with their drinks, and they nabbed a few chickens and a rooster from a neighboring Tory farmer. In honor of the feast, they garnished their glasses with the rooster's plucked tail feathers and toasted each other. A great American institution—the cocktail hour—was born.

That's one story, anyway. Other explanations are somewhat more prosaic. "Cocktail" could be a Yankee corruption of *decota*, the Latin word for "distilled water." Or it could come from New Orleans, where an eggcup called a "coquetier" was used to measure out liquor. Or it could have originated even farther south, in Latin America, where native people used a root from a plant the Spanish called the *cola de gallo* ("cock's tail") to stir fermented beverages.

The first printed definition of cocktail appeared on May 13, 1806, in the Hudson, New York, newspaper *The Balance and Colombian Repository*: "Cock-tail, then, is a stimulating liquor composed of spirits of any kind, sugar, water, and bitters." With an occasional dash of politics, too, for the editor noted, "[It] is supposed to be an excellent electioneering potion...because, a person having swallowed a glass of it, is ready to swallow anything else."

There seem to be as many theories about the genesis of the cocktail as there are variations on the drink itself. One thing most historians agree on, however, is that cocktails are a uniquely American innovation. "Professor" Jerry Thomas, who is often hailed as the father of American mixology, included dozens of cocktail recipes in his 1862 bartender's guide *How to Mix Drinks*. He offered brandy, gin, champagne, whiskey, and rum cocktails, both plain and fancy; a "Jersey Cocktail," made from hard cider; and an alcohol-free version with soda and a twist of lemon.

So drink up! No matter where the name comes from, cocktails are as American as apple pie and the Fourth of July. They're the perfect libation for our multicultural, mix-it-up nation.

Q How do dictionary writers know how to spell a word?

A How would you know if they didn't? Dictionary writers are generally a bunch of respected scholars and smart people who are each hired to edit small sections of the work (say, all the words from "ban-" to "bec-"). Not surprisingly, editing a dictionary generally requires a large amount of time devoted to reading—anything and everything. Dictionary editors might scan whatever they read for new words that are becoming popular, new uses of old words, and any spelling variants. Once that's done, the entries might be recorded in a massive database, and perhaps kept in hard copy. This database can provide an easy reference for research about words.

A word is usually not added to the dictionary until a determination has been made that it is widely used by various sources. The choice of spelling is based on all the examples, with the most common spelling being the one used. The dictionary may also have general "house rules" about how to spell words.

Dictionary editors have some discretion in choosing spellings. An example of this is the American spelling of "color" compared to the British spelling, "colour," which goes back to Noah Webster, editor of the first American dictionary. One of Webster's pet peeves was when a word appeared to have a misleading or overly complicated spelling—too many silent letters, for example. He believed that American spelling should reflect the values of the new republic, emphasizing logical consistency and spartan simplicity. In this instance, he tried to reform the spelling by dropping the "u" from the word and others like it ("humour," for example, became "humor"). The public ran with it, and the spelling stuck. This wasn't the case, however, with some of his other proposed reforms, such as "tung" for "tongue" and "wimmen" for "women."

Now that the printed word is ubiquitous, there are fewer spelling variations than in the distant past, when scribes would typically try to spell words according to what they heard, with no dictionaries—and certainly no Google—for checking the hard ones. Still, today's dictionary writers have their work cut out for them. By some estimates, the English language has between 750,000 and 1,250,000 words.

Q How do people break concrete blocks with their hands?

A In a face-off between hand and block, the hand has a surprising advantage: Bone is significantly stronger than concrete. In fact, bone can withstand about forty times more stress than concrete before reaching its breaking point. What's more, the surrounding muscles and ligaments in your hands are good stress absorbers, making the hand and arm one tough weapon. So if you position your hand correctly, you're not going to break it by hitting concrete.

The trick to smashing a block is thrusting this sturdy mass into the concrete with enough force to bend the block beyond its breaking point. The force of any impact is determined by the momentum of the two objects in the collision. Momentum is a multiple of the mass and velocity of an object.

When striking an object, the speed of your blow is critical. You also have to hit the block with a relatively small area of your hand, so that the force of the impact is focused in one spot on the block—this concentrates the stress on the concrete. As in golf, the only way for a martial arts student to hit accurately with greater speed is practice, practice, practice.

But there is a basic mental trick involved: You have to overcome your natural instinct to slow your strike as your hand approaches the block. Martial arts masters concentrate on an impact spot beyond the block, so that the hand is still at maximum speed when it makes contact with the concrete. You also need to put as much body mass as you can into the strike; this can be achieved by twisting your body and lowering your torso as you make contact. A black belt in karate can throw a chop at about forty-six feet per second, which results in a force of about 2,800 newtons. (A newton is the unit of force needed to accelerate a mass.) That's more than enough power to break the standard one-and-a-half-inch concrete slabs that are commonly used in demonstrations and typically can withstand only 1,900 newtons. Nonetheless, while hands are dandy in a block-breaking exhibition, you'll find that for sidewalk demolition and other large projects, jackhammers are really the way to go.

Q How many kids have had an eye put out by a BB gun?

A In any BB gun discussion, anywhere in the Western world (presumably), it's only a matter of time before someone quotes *A Christmas Story*. Ralphie, the movie's main character, wants nothing on Earth so much as a BB gun. But every time he voices his desire, his mother has five words for him: "You'll shoot your eye out!" The line has become a mantra for concerned mothers—a classic BB gun block. When it comes to real kids in real backyards shooting real BB guns, how plausible is this concern?

Unfortunately for every ten-year-old who has ever petitioned his parents for one of these toy rifles, his mother's concern is somewhat justified. According to a report filed by the Centers for Disease Control and Prevention, there were more than forty-seven thousand BB gun-related injuries to children and teenagers treated in emergency rooms across the country between June 1992 and May 1994. Of these, 2,839 (about 6 percent) involved an injury to the eye. It's a rather small figure compared to injuries sustained to the arms, legs, hands, and feet, however; shots to the extremities comprised 54 percent of the reported injuries.

As famous as the mantra has become, shots to the eye are not the only ones to cause serious harm. There have been cases of BBs penetrating deep enough to become lodged in vital organs, and a report issued in 2004 quotes an average of four deaths a year due to BB guns and other nonpowder rifles (those that fire by use of a spring, pressurized CO_2, or pressurized air).

BB guns can be harmless toys when used properly, under the supervision of a mature adult, but their dangerous aspects should not be downplayed. Use of safety glasses and thick, protective clothing can reduce the risk of injury, but teaching safe conduct and respect for guns (even when they only fire BBs) is the best way to avoid a trip to the local emergency room.

More than three million nonpowder rifles are sold every year. Many are sold in department stores and toy stores, and many are sold to kids. Most states have no age restrictions when it comes to the sale of BB guns. If these kids are not taught to respect their guns, it may not be long before the toys are banned altogether. In fact, the state of New York has already done so.

"You'll shoot your eye out!" may be the easiest way to shoot down a ten-year-old's dream of owning a BB gun, but it's one of the least likely outcomes. Not every child with a BB gun is going to injure himself. And, in the event of an injury, it's much more likely that the BB will end up lodged in an extremity. Maybe the mantra should be changed to, "You'll shoot your palm and end up with a metal ball trapped just below the skin for the rest of your life."

On second thought, we like the other phrase better.

Q How deep are the oceans?

A First, the boring answer. Going by average depth, the Pacific Ocean is the deepest: 13,740 feet. The Indian and Atlantic oceans are a close second and third at 12,740 and 12,254 feet deep, respectively. The Arctic Ocean is relatively shallow—3,407 feet at its deepest point.

But there's much more to the story. The terrain of the land that lies beneath the oceans is just as varied as the terrain of the higher and drier parts of the globe. The ocean floors have their own mountain ranges—the tallest of which poke through the waves to become islands—and they also have plunging valleys called trenches.

These trenches mark the seams at which the earth's tectonic plates come together. Movement of these plates forces one under the other in a process called subduction. Trenches can be narrow, but they run the entire lengths of the tectonic plates.

Trenches are the deepest parts of the oceans—and the deepest of all the trenches is the Mariana Trench, which is named for its proximity to the Mariana Islands, which are located in the Pacific Ocean between Australia and Japan. The depth of the Mariana

Trench varies considerably along its 1,580 miles, but oceanographers have identified one part that's deeper than the others—in other words, the deepest part of the deepest trench in the deepest ocean on the planet. This place is called the Challenger Deep.

The bottom of this valley in the ocean floor is a bone-crushing 35,810 feet deep—almost seven miles below sea level. One way to illustrate this depth is to say that if we wanted to hide Mount Everest—the entire thing—they could toss it into the Challenger Deep. Once it had settled on the bottom, there would still be more than a mile of water between the highest point of the mountain and the ocean's surface.

The Challenger Deep, discovered in 1951, was named for the first vessel to pinpoint the deepest part of the trench: HMS *Challenger II*, manned by Jacques Piccard. The first vessel to plumb these depths was the U.S. Naval submersible *Trieste* in 1960, manned by Piccard and U.S. Navy Lt. Don Walsh. Hydrostatic pressure, caused by the accumulated weight of the water above you, increases as you descend into a body of water. At the bottom of the Challenger Deep, the *Trieste* had to withstand eight tons of pressure per square inch. Bone-crushing, indeed.

Q How come male and female shirts have buttons on opposite sides?

A Despite the many strides the feminist movement has made over the past few decades, there is simply no denying that men and women are biologically different (except in certain red-light-district shows, which we've never, ever seen).

Clothing has developed in ways to accommodate these differences. Some make sense (we'd wager that you've never seen women's underwear sporting that little flap/vent thing). But putting buttons on opposite sides of the shirt? Why?

Although it might seem ridiculous for men's and women's shirts to have buttons on opposite sides—most people are right-handed, and it is far easier to manipulate a button with your dominant hand—scholars point to fashion history to explain how this came to be.

Buttons have been around for thousands of years, but they served no purpose other than being decorative until about the thirteenth century. That's when the functional button (and, just as important-ly, the buttonhole) was invented, sending European nobility into a veritable button frenzy. Buttons became a symbol of both status and fashion, appearing everywhere and anywhere, often unneces-sarily.

Perhaps the apex of button-mania came in the sixteenth century with the button-loving king of France, Francis I. In 1520, Francis planned a meeting with the English king, Henry VIII, in hopes of arranging a military alliance. Wanting desperately to impress Henry, Francis thought long and hard about how to strike the right chord.

It was the sort of situation that required the utmost tact and states-manship; the sort of situation that needed the grace and intelli-gence befitting the ruler of one of the world's greatest powers; the sort of situation, Francis tragically decided, that demanded he wear a velvet suit adorned with more than thirteen thousand gold buttons. There is no record of Henry's reaction, though it goes without saying that no alliance was formed.

Francis's ill-fated wardrobe decision also gives us insight into our original question. For a long time, buttons were too costly to appear on anything except the garments of the nobility. Because noble ladies were dressed by their servants, it was the obvious choice to put the buttons on the left side, making it easier for the right-handed servants to button their mistresses. Men dressed themselves, and so their buttons went on the right.

According to historians, there is no real reason for men's and women's buttons to persist in their opposition—it continues out of tradition. Thankfully, that's the only button tradition Francis and his contemporaries bequeathed to us.

Q How do worms breathe?

A Worms spend most of their lives underground, but they don't burrow in the traditional sense. Unlike most "underground" creatures, worms don't make tunnel systems and dens—instead, they squish, slide, and squirm through the soil, leaving nary a trace of their presence. Since they don't create any more room than they need for themselves in the earth, how is it possible for them to breathe? There can't be much air down there.

A worm lacks the accoutrements that are typically associated with breathing (i.e., a mouth, a nose, lungs). It breathes by taking in oxygen through the pores in its skin. To make this possible, the worm's skin must be moist. (This is why, after it rains, worms that are stranded on the sidewalk perish before they can get back into the soil—the sun dries them right out, suffocating them.) Oxygen is absorbed by the capillaries that line the surface of a worm's slimy skin; from there, it goes straight into the bloodstream. In mammals, this process is longer by one step: They take oxygen into their lungs, where it is then transferred to the bloodstream.

Worms can survive underwater for a sustained period of time, but their pores don't function the same way a fish's gills do, so a submerged worm will eventually drown. Some scientists believe that this is why worms come to the surface during a rainstorm: The soil becomes too wet and threatens to drown them. Of course, as we mentioned, this pilgrimage to the surface can lead to a different set of problems.

It seems that the key to a worm's longevity is to successfully squirm the fine line between too little and too much moisture. That, and avoiding the pinching fingers of anglers and curious kids.

Q How do hurricanes get their names?

A Hurricanes are given their names by an agency of the United Nations called the World Meteorological Organization (WMO). The staff of the WMO doesn't spend its days thumbing through baby books trying to pick the perfect name for each newborn storm; instead, it uses a system to assign the names automatically. At the start of each year's stormy season, staffers dust off an alphabetical list of twenty-one names—one for each of the letters except Q, U, X, Y, and Z (these letters are never used due to the scarcity of names that begin with them). As a tropical storm develops, the WMO assigns it the next name on the list, working from A to W and alternating between male and female names. There are six such lists; the WMO rotates through them so that the names repeat every six years.

These lists aren't set in stone, though. If a hurricane causes serious destruction, its name is usually retired. If a hard-hit country requests that a name be replaced, the WMO picks a substitute for that letter of the alphabet. For example, in 2005 Katrina was replaced with Katia, which will next appear in the 2011 rotation. When the WMO picks a new name, the only requirements are that it must be short and distinct, easy to pronounce, generally familiar, and not offensive.

It's not clear who started the tradition of naming hurricanes, but it predates the WMO by hundreds of years. The custom goes back at least to the eighteenth century, when people in the Caribbean began to name storms after the nearest saint's day. For example, the 1876 hurricane that struck Puerto Rico was called Hurricane San Felipe. A more personalized approach was taken by an Austra-lian meteorologist in the late nineteenth century: He named storms for mythological figures, women, and politicians that he didn't like—but that idea never really caught wind worldwide.

Our current method of naming storms was first formalized by the U.S. National Hurricane Center in 1953, after several naming schemes that used latitude and longitude coordinates and pho-netic alphabet signs—the "Able, Baker, Charlie" type of code that's used by the military—proved to be too confusing. At first, storms were given only women's names; this convention was attributed to World War II soldiers who reportedly named storms after their wives.

By the 1970s, women understandably felt that it was sexist to link their gender with the destructive forces of tropical storms, so in 1979 the WMO added male names to the lists. Next thing you know, women are going to demand that half of the storms be referred to as "himmicanes," too.

Q How many Ronald McDonalds have there been?

A McDonald's guards this bit of information even more closely than its secret sauce recipe. The company won't even acknowledge the existence of multiple Ronalds, though McDonald's obviously would need many actors to keep up with store openings, hospital visits, and other events around the world. The company forbids Ronald actors from revealing what they do.

The only specific Ronald actor that McDonald's happily acknowledges is the original one, Willard Scott, who went on to become the world's most famous weatherman. The story began in 1960, when Scott played Bozo the Clown in the Washington, D.C., version of *Bozo's Circus*. A local McDonald's franchisee sponsored the show, and Scott also appeared as Bozo at McDonald's restaurants as part of the promotion. He was a big hit, so when the station dropped *Bozo's Circus* in 1963, a franchisee hired Scott to play a new McDonald's clown character in local ads.

The ads were a success, and McDonald's decided in 1965 to feature the character in nationwide TV spots as part of its sponsorship of the Macy's Thanksgiving Day parade. Instead of using Scott, McDonald's hired a thinner actor, reasoning that it would be easier to find lean actors rather than heavy actors to play Ronald around the nation. (Guess the obesity epidemic hadn't yet gripped America.)

The history gets fuzzy there, but we know that McDonald's was working through the 1970s on building its clown army. In 1972 the company published *Ronald and How*, a training manual for new Ronalds. In a 2003 *Wall Street Journal* article, marketing experts who were familiar with McDonald's said that there were about two hundred fifty active Ronalds around the world, which could mean that there have been several thousand over the years. Every two years, current Ronalds and prospective Ronalds attend a secret Ronald McDonald convention, where they have to pass inspection. It's heady stuff, to be sure.

Scott is the only person confirmed by McDonald's to have appeared as Ronald in television ads. There are Internet rumors about other TV Ronalds, but these actors are unconfirmed. Mayor McCheese could not be reached for comment.

Q How come deer freeze in headlights?

A It is a universal human moment: You're stunned, confused, and blown into a state of complete disarray, and all you can do is stand there silently and motionlessly. Witnesses agree: You were caught like a deer in the headlights.

We all know what it means, and some of us have even seen the inspiration for this adage firsthand, so the obvious question is why? Why does a deer that is surprised by the lights of an oncoming car freeze in the middle of the road and seem to wait for the impact?

There are a couple of scientific theories concerning this phenomenon. (Neither has anything to do with depression, suicidal tendencies among forest fauna, or a masculine desire to display bravery by playing chicken in traffic.) These theories attribute the animal's reaction to instinct.

According to the first explanation, the deer presumes that anything it doesn't recognize is a predator. It stops moving to reduce the risk of being seen and waits for the predator to move on or give chase. Unfortunately, when the "predator" is a set of vehicle headlights, standing still for any amount of time is a bad idea, and the deer will often wind up as roadkill.

The other theory posits that the deer is temporarily stricken with a sort of blindness that is caused by powerful high-beam headlamps. Since a deer lacks the cognitive ability to understand why the forest, grass, sky, and road have all disappeared, it simply freezes because there's nowhere to go. While the animal is waiting for its sight to be restored... *wham!* Roadkill. If the deer is lucky, its revenge is a totaled hatchback and a stranded commuter. Nevertheless, that's hardly an even score: one dead, and one terribly inconvenienced.

If you ever find the road blocked by a frozen deer, there are some ways to get the animal moving again. Blinking your lights, flashing your brights, or honking your horn will often startle the deer into movement. Don't attempt to swerve around the animal; this may spin you out of control and into oncoming traffic or the nearest tree. Instead, hit the brakes while doing the aforementioned blinking, flashing, and/or honking, and hope that the deer comes to its senses. Otherwise—*wham!*—it'll be roadkill.

Q How come old ladies have blue hair?

A Black knee socks with sandals. Pants hiked to the armpits. Wraparound sunglasses enveloping half the face like something out of a low-budget science-fiction movie. As we get older, our hearing fails, our eyesight wanes, and our bodies crumble, but perhaps nothing collapses more dramatically than our sense of fashion. Some of these fashion abominations arise from practicality; others exist because older people simply don't care. But blue hair? Surely that's not by design, is it?

Don't worry—Grandma hasn't suddenly embraced punk culture. Ironically, though, while most style disasters of the elderly stem from fashion apathy, blue hair comes from trying too hard. As everyone knows, our hair turns gray as we age. That's because the hair's pigment cells, which produce the melanin that gives hair its color, don't live quite as long as the average human body. As the pigment cells die, the melanin dissipates, leaving the hair a silvery or white color.

Unfortunately, in our modern age, it also leaves the hair partially yellow, thanks to the decades of pollution and chemicals to which we have been subjected. In order to combat this, many commercial rinses include a blue dye that, in theory, negates the yellowing and turns the hair a lovely silver color. However, these rinses sometimes have too much blue dye or are inappropriately applied, leaving the hair tinted blue and making Grandma look like she just emerged from a Ramones show at CBGB.

As with other fashion quirks of senior citizens, it's best to simply kiss Grandma on the cheek and compliment her on her new hairdo regardless of its hue. God willing, she doesn't even realize it's blue.

Q How do chameleons change color?

A They haven't mastered plaid or paisley, and they don't do personalized messages, but chameleons can pull off some pretty impressive colored stripes when the mood strikes them. How many animals can say that?

Chameleons accomplish this trick by manipulating specialized coloration cells called chromatophores, which lie beneath the protective outer layer of skin, or epidermis. A chameleon's chromatophores are arranged in three layers—yellow (xanthophores), dark brown or black (melanophores), and red (erythrophores). As these pigmented cells contract, their colors become more concentrated and interact to create complex, varied patterns of color.

But that's just half of the story. There's another layer of cells, called iridocytes, that lies between the epidermis and the chromatophores. Unlike the chromatophores, the iridocytes do not contain pigment of their own; instead, these cells contribute to coloration by diffusing and directing the sunlight as it permeates the chameleon's skin. Depending on the position of the iridocytes, they can intensify or weaken the illumination of the chromatophores.

The iridocytes also add their own unique sheen to the chameleon's palette, thanks to a phenomenon called the Tyndall effect. When the iridocytes scatter light, the blue wavelengths are diffused more strongly. This can create the appearance of an almost iridescent blue tint, which is often called Tyndall blue. (This is the same phenomenon that makes the sky blue on a clear day.)

So how do chameleons control their colorful displays? In a way, they don't. Their pigmented cells expand and contract in response to hormones that work with the autonomic nervous system—the "automatic" part of the brain that regulates heart rate and breathing, as well as involuntary responses like blushing, sweating, and sexual arousal.

So what's the point of this color-changing? There's a common belief that this ability helps chameleons camouflage themselves, but it's a misconception. In the chameleon's natural environment, there aren't many brilliant red and yellow backgrounds, so a shade of green usually does just fine for blending in. As it turns out, color-changing primarily serves other purposes.

One of these functions is regulating body temperature. If a chameleon needs to warm up, it may change to a darker color that absorbs more light. More often, though, color changes serve to indicate the chameleon's mood, which is handy for lizard-to-lizard communication.

For example, two male chameleons that are competing for the company of a fair lady may hold a color contest, showcasing their best and brightest designs. The loser will return to a boring grayish green and slink off, while the winner will strut its red-striped stuff all over town.

Some chameleons also seem to change color to let other chameleons know that there are predators in the area. If they could only learn to display corporate logos, they'd be able to make some serious cash and move somewhere safer.

Q How far do you have to dive underwater to escape gunfire?

A Unlike outrunning an explosion, this action-hero escape plan actually works. A 2005 episode of the Discovery Channel's *MythBusters* proved that bullets fired into the water at an angle will slow to a safe speed at fewer than four feet below the surface. In fact, bullets from some high-powered guns in this test basically disintegrated on the water's surface.

It might seem counterintuitive that speeding bullets don't penetrate water as easily as something slow, like a diving human being or a falling anchor. But it makes sense. Water has considerable mass, so when anything hits it, it pushes back. The force of the impact is equal to the change in momentum (momentum is velocity times mass) divided by the time taken to change the momentum.

In other words, the faster the object is going, the more its momentum will change when it hits, and the greater the force of impact will be. For the same reason that a car suffers more damage in a head-on collision with a wall at fifty miles per hour than at five miles per hour, a speeding bullet takes a bigger hit than something that is moving more slowly.

The initial impact slows the bullet considerably, and the drag that's created as it moves through water brings it to a stop. The impact on faster-moving bullets is even greater, so they are more likely to break apart or slow to a safe speed within the first few feet of water.

The worst-case scenario is if someone fires a low-powered gun at you straight down into the water. In the *MythBusters* episode, one of the tests involved firing a nine-millimeter pistol directly down into a block of underwater ballistics gel. Eight feet below the surface seemed to be the safe distance—the ballistics gel showed that the impact from the bullet wouldn't have been fatal at this depth. But if a shot from the same gun were fired at a thirty-degree angle (which would be a lot more likely if you were fleeing from shooters on shore), you'd be safe at just four feet down.

The problem with this escape plan is that you have to pop up sooner or later to breathe, and the shooter on shore will be ready. But if you are a proper action hero, you can hold your breath for at least ten minutes, which is plenty of time to swim to your top-secret submarine car.

Q How is it that you stop noticing a smell after a while?

A We should thank our lucky stars for this phenomenon—it makes public transportation a lot more bearable, and it surely has saved countless marriages. And back in our hunter-gatherer days, it made the sense of smell a very effective survival tool.

To understand why, we need to review the fundamentals of smelling. When you smell something, you're detecting floating molecules that were cast off from all the stuff around you. Inside your nose, you have millions of olfactory sensory neurons, each of which has eight to twenty hair-like cilia that extend into a layer of mucus. These cilia have receptors that detect molecules floating into the nose. Different receptors are sensitive to different types of molecules; for example, when a grass molecule makes its way into your nose, you don't detect it until it bumps into one of the receptors that is sensitive to that particular type of molecule. This neuron then sends a signal to a part of the brain called the olfactory bulb, which is devoted to making sense of odors.

Based on the type of receptors that have been activated, your brain tells you what kinds of molecules are wafting into your nose. You perceive this information as a unique smell. If many sensory neurons fire in response to the same type of molecule, you experience a more intense smell.

This is a handy tool in the wild because it helps you find good food, avoid bad food, and sense predators. And it works a lot better if you're able to filter out ongoing odors that are particularly pungent. For example, you would have a much harder time sniffing out delicious but distant bananas in the jungle if you were preoccupied by the pervasive smell of fetid mud. And since we animals are a naturally stinky bunch, our own body odors would drown out all kinds of useful smells if we didn't possess a means to ignore them.

It's not clear exactly how this happens, but biologists believe that it occurs at both the receptor level and inside the brain. In other words, sensory neurons in the nose reduce their sensitivities to particular types of molecules, while the brain stops paying attention to whatever indications it receives regarding those odors. This filtering process is most likely the driving force behind long-term desensitization to a certain smell.

It's why a factory worker might stop noticing a strong chemical smell. Or why a wife doesn't run for cover when her husband takes off his shoes after a long day.

Q How exactly does one get off the schneid?

A Winning a game is good. Winning a series is better. But there's almost nothing that brings more relief to an athlete or sports fan than getting off the schneid. This strange phrase, which is popular in sports journalism, means breaking a losing streak or ending a run of poor luck. Some teams are more attached to the schneid than others: Chicago Cubs fans, for example, have watched as their team has stayed firmly glued to the schneid for over a century. But what the heck is a schneid, anyway?

It's short for schneider—not the surname made famous by the handyman from the classic sitcom *One Day at a Time*, but the German word *schneider*, which means "tailor." So the question should be, "How exactly do you get off a tailor? And while we're at it, how did you get on this tailor in the first place?"

As you might expect, the tailor in question is at best metaphorical, and the term has taken a somewhat circuitous route to modern-day sports fans. The story begins in nineteenth-century Germany, when a card game known as skat was sweeping the land. A distant relation to trump games like hearts and spades, skat consists of sets totaling one hundred twenty points. In order to win a game of skat, a player needs to garner at least sixty-one of these points. While failing to score sixty points earns a loss, failing to score even thirty points, besides being embarrassing, also earns the hapless loser the moniker "schneider."

Several explanations for this dubious honorific have been put forth. The first is that tailors were often poor, so a poverty of skat points would naturally invoke an association with these craftsmen of meager means. A second theory, which was suggested by early skat expert E. E. Lemcke in his 1886 skat rulebook, is that players who earned fewer than thirty points were first called *geschnitten*, which means "cut" or "sliced." Eventually, through verbal association, the sliced—*geschnitten*—turned into the slicers—*schneiders*—or, literally, the tailors.

Before *schneider* could be co-opted by American sports journalists, the term had to make its way into the American lexicon. This happened via another card game, gin rummy, which adopted schneider to describe a player who scores zero points. Though younger Americans might find gin rummy a bit dull compared to *Guitar Hero*, it was enormously popular for much of the first half of the twentieth century. Therefore, it was only natural that some enterprising sports journalist would borrow from its lexicon to spice up an article.

The first written use of the phrase we could find is from an August 1960 United Press International article claiming that American Olympic divers who captured gold medals in Rome got the Americans "off the schneid." Eventually, just about everyone gets off the schneid, which probably offers little solace to Cubs fans. For these long-suffering folks, we'll pull out another sports cliché and tell them to take it "one day at a time."

Q How do you pay through the nose?

A Very painfully. Actually, although philologists don't agree on a definitive answer, the phrase "pay through the nose," meaning to pay an exorbitant or unfair price for something, may have its origin in an excruciating procedure. According to one etymology, the unusual phrase dates back to the ninth-century occupation of Ireland by Denmark. The Danes, apparently, were far harsher then than they are now, and instituted something referred to as a "nose tax." Any Irishman who didn't pay this tax would be punished by having his nose slit open.

While this is an entertaining—if brutal—theory, it seems unlikely, largely because the phrase "pay through the nose" didn't appear in written English until well into the sixteen hundreds, some seven hundred years later. With this in mind, a second etymology, which is equally unprovable but much more logical, ties the phrase to the word *rhino*, which appeared in the sixteen hundreds as a slang term for money. Because *rhino* is Greek for "nose" (people used a lot more erudite slang back in the day, apparently), the terms worked themselves into a common phrase.

A third possibility suggests that "pay through the nose" is associated with the term "bleeding," as in "you're bleeding me dry." The use of "bleed" in reference to money first appeared in the English language at roughly the same time as "pay through the nose," and so perhaps it was the symbol of a nosebleed—both persistent and often unfair—that became associated with outrageous expenditures.

Though the phrase "pay through the nose" may have lost its original erudite associations, the idiom is still alive and well—especially around tax time, when millions of Americans complain about the IRS "bleeding them dry." But Americans actually have it pretty good. It's not like IRS agents are ninth-century Danes or anything . . . even if the tax forms do seem to be written in an ancient, dead language.

Q How many human languages are there?

A *Moi! Natya! Malo! O-si-yo!* That's hello in Finnish, Kikuyu, Samoan, and Cherokee, respectively. How many different languages are there? By one count: 6,912. That's a lot of hellos. It's also a lot of good-byes: Nearly five hundred of these languages have fewer than one hundred fluent speakers and are in danger of dying out within a generation.

By contrast, Mandarin Chinese is spoken by about 1.05 billion people. This includes both the 882 million native speakers and 178 million who speak it as a second language, adding up to nearly a sixth of the world's population. Hindi/Urdu or Hindustani, the primary language of the subcontinent of India, is spoken natively by 451 million people and by another 453 million as a second language. English comes in third with 337 million native speakers, plus 350 million who use it as a second language.

At the bottom of the list are Comanche, a Native American language with only two hundred fluent speakers; Livonian, a Latvian language spoken by thirty-five people; and varoius Sami dialects from the reindeer-herding tribes of northern Scandinavia with fewer than forty speakers each.

Who's counting languages, and why? For many years, the *Ethnologue* has been the most reliable source of information on world languages. This organization, started by Christian missionaries who were interested in translating the Bible into every known language, partnered with the International Organization for Standardization in 2002 to create a coding system for tracking languages. Recently, the *Observatoire de Linguistique*, a European research network, and *Encarta*, the encyclopedia published by Microsoft, have also released their own language indices.

Not all of these sources agree. There may be as few as five thousand languages or as many as eleven thousand, depending on which method linguists use to distinguish dialects from full-fledged languages. They all reach the same conclusion, however: As the globe's population increases, the number of unique languages decreases. Every language, no matter how obscure, represents part of humanity's cultural inheritance. Some researchers have concluded that half the world's current languages will die out by the end of the twenty-first century, taking much of their history, music, and literature with them.

Fortunately, the future of linguistic diversity may not be that dire. Languages can demonstrate surprising resiliency. Witness the persistence of Yiddish. Not so dead yet, *nu*? However, Walmajarri (Australia, one thousand speakers), Inuinnaqtun (Canada, two thousand speakers), and Culina (Peru/Brazil, 1,300 speakers) may not be so lucky.

Maybe we should all brush up on our language skills before it's too late. Get a bilingual dictionary, take a deep breath, and learn how to say, "Hello."

Q How do fruit flies find fruit?

A Fruit flies appear around fruit so often that people once believed that the insects were generated by the fruit itself. This theory, called spontaneous generation, was famously debunked by the French chemist Louis Pasteur in the 1850s when he sealed a glass dome over a plate of fruit. *Voilà!* No fruit flies.

Indeed, with its fantastic fertility rate and short life span, the tiny *Drosophila melanogaster* has proved to be a model organism for genetic researchers. It's being studied even today by computer engineers. More on that later, but first: How do the flies find the fruit?

Smell is one way. Fruit flies are attracted by the odor of fermentation; it's why they're also called vinegar flies. However, fruit flies don't have a great sense of smell—compared to humans, they have 80 percent fewer olfactory receptors. So fruit flies employ additional senses to find food, and vision is their chief asset. A fruit fly's eyes are among the most highly developed in the insect world. Each fly has approximately eight hundred separate eye units, and more than half of its brainpower is devoted to visual processing.

But the fly's brain is so tiny that scientists used to wonder if it was capable of processing more than one source of sensory information at a time. In other words, does a fruit fly have trouble using its sense of smell and its sense of vision simultaneously?

In 2007, Mark Frye of the UCLA Brain Research Institute tested how well flies were able to track an odor in the presence of both a high-contrast background and a neutral gray one. The superior performance of the flies against the bright background proved that they do coordinate their sense of vision with their sense of smell to navigate to food.

Why is this important? Computer engineers are trying to develop robots that are capable of utilizing more than one source of information when performing complex tasks. Learning how organisms with small brains, such as fruit flies, integrate sensory input might help these engineers to develop new and better circuitry for artificially intelligent beings.

So, the tiny fruit fly is making a mighty contribution to science. You may not like it when fruit flies buzz around your peaches, but before you shoo them away, perhaps you should say, "Thank you."

Q How does water make your skin pruned?

A When you spend enough time in water, the skin on your feet and hands gets wrinkled, or "pruned." No, it doesn't age you: If it did, there would be a lot of filthy people around, clinging to their youth. After you get out of water, your skin eventually returns to normal. The reason for this has to do with how our skin is composed.

Skin is made up of three layers. The deepest layer is subcutaneous tissue that includes fat, nerves, and connective tissue. The second layer is the dermis, where you find your sweat glands, hair roots, nerves, and blood vessels. The top layer (the wrinkle-maker) is the epidermis. The surface—or top outer layer—of the epidermis is made of dead keratin cells. Keratin, which is also part of finger-nails, is there to protect the rest of the skin. Your hands and feet have the thickest layers of keratin; since you use these appendages all the time, they need to have an extra protective coating. We couldn't do much if the skin on our hands and feet was as thin as that on our eyelids.

So what happens when you go for a swim or soak in the tub?

The keratin absorbs a lot of water. In order to make room for it all, wrinkles form and the skin plumps. Why wrinkling as opposed to just plain ol' swelling? Because the top layer is connected to the other layers of skin, but in an uneven manner. The bottom layers of skin are more watertight than the top layer, so the water has to sit there for a while before it can be absorbed. Water that is not absorbed by the skin will evaporate, which returns your skin to normal.

The rest of your skin doesn't have such a thick layer of keratin, so it isn't as wrinkle-prone. The rest of your body also has hair, at the base of which are glands that secrete an oil called sebum. The sebum coats the hair follicles. We all know how oil and water react—the non-hand and non-feet skin does not absorb as much water. Therefore, the rest of you stays wrinkle-free.

Q How did Europe divvy up the New World?

A Initially, it was really quite simple: The pope decided who got what. In 1493—one year after Christopher Columbus's first voyage—the largely Catholic kingdoms of Spain and Portugal were the only European players in the New World. Other countries were decades away from investigating the strange land; the Pilgrims wouldn't arrive at Plymouth Rock for more than a century.

Ferdinand and Isabella of Spain had financed Columbus's voyage and figured that they had an obvious claim to the lands he had discovered. But Portugal's King John II disagreed. He cited the fourteen-year-old Treaty of Alcaçovas, drafted when Portugal was exploring the coast of Africa. The treaty, which Spain had signed, gave Portugal all lands south of the Canary Islands. The New World was south of the Canaries, so it belonged to Portugal. Columbus, according to John, was trespassing on his land.

Isabella and Ferdinand of Spain were indignant. They brought up a law that dated back to the Crusades that said Christian rulers could seize control of any heathen land in order to spread the Catholic faith. *So there.* Rather than go to war, they asked the pope to resolve the issue because, frankly, Portugal had a big, powerful navy and Spain did not. (No one bothered to ask the native people in the New World what they had to say about this, in case you're wondering.)

Pope Alexander VI, of the infamous Borgia family, drew a line from the North Pole to the South Pole, one hundred leagues west of the Cape Verde Islands, which was the site of a Portuguese colony. Portugal received every heathen land east of that line: the Azores, the Canary Islands, Africa (including Madagascar), and Saudi Arabia. Years later, explorers found that the north-south line went right through South America; this gave Portugal a chunk of that continent as well. That's why most Brazilians speak Portuguese to this day.

Spain got everything to the west of the pope's line. In 1494, when the treaty was signed at Tordesillas, no one realized that the majority of two huge continents sat in Spain's portion. Isabella and Ferdinand thought that they were getting only the puny Caribbean islands that Columbus had spotted. In fact, they were upset and felt cheated, but the pope's decision was final.

At least for a while. A later treaty changed the line, and then the British, French, Russians, and Dutch got in on the action and began claiming parts of the New World for themselves. The Treaty of Tordesillas was forgotten.

Q How can celebrity tabloids get away with publishing obviously untrue stories?

A Supermarket tabloids thrive on publishing outlandish celebrity rumors and innuendo. You'd think that the subjects of their articles would be suing them all the time. How in the world could the tabloids survive the legal fees and multi-million-dollar judgments? The truth is, if tabloids are good at one thing, it's surviving.

There are two kinds of tabloids: the ridiculous ones that publish stories nobody really believes ("Bigfoot Cured My Arthritis!") and those that focus on celebrity gossip.

The ridiculous stories are easy to get away with. They're mostly fabricated or based on slender truths. As long as they contain nothing damaging about a real person, there's no one to file a lawsuit. Bigfoot isn't litigious.

Celebrity gossip is trickier. To understand how tabloids avoid legal problems, we need to learn a little bit about the legal definition of "libel." To be found guilty of libel, you must have published something about another person that is provably false.

Moreover, the falsehood has to have caused that person some kind of damage, even if only his or her reputation is harmed. If the subject of the story is a notable person, such as a politician or a movie star, libel legally occurs only if publication of the falsehood is malicious. This means that the publisher knows the information is false, had access to the truth but ignored it, and published the information anyway.

Tabloids generally have lawyers on staff or on retainer who are experts in media law and libel. By consulting with their lawyers, tabloid editors can publish stories that get dangerously close to libel but don't quite cross the line.

One defense against libel is publication of the truth: You can't sue someone for saying something about you that's true, no matter how embarrassing it may be. And tabloids know that if they print something close to the truth, a celebrity is unlikely to sue because a trial could reveal a skeleton in the closet that's even more embarrassing.

Libel lawyers also know that a tabloid is in the clear if it publishes a story based on an informant's opinion. Opinions can't be disproved, so they don't meet the criteria for libel. This explains headlines such as this: "Former Housekeeper Says Movie Star Joe Smith Is a Raving Lunatic!" As long as the tabloid makes a token effort to corroborate the story—or even includes a rebuttal of the housekeeper's claims within the article—it is fairly safe from a legal standpoint.

Of course, legal tricks don't always work. Some movie stars, musicians, and other celebrities have successfully sued tabloids for tens of millions of dollars. That tabloids continue to thrive despite such judgments shows just how much money there is to be made in the rumors-and-innuendo business.

Q How have the Russians preserved Lenin's body?

A On January 21, 1924, Soviet leader Vladimir Lenin died after a series of strokes. Two days later, pathologist Alexei Abrikosov embalmed Lenin's body so it would be presentable for viewing. A makeshift wooden tomb was designed and built by architect Alexey Schusev on Red Square by the Kremlin Wall in Moscow. More than one hundred thousand people visited the tomb within a month and a half.

By August, people were still coming to pay their respects to the man who had spearheaded the Bolshevik Revolution in Russia and brought about Communist rule. Scientists Vladimir Vorbiov, Boris Zbarsky, and others routinely reintroduced the preservative chemicals into Lenin's body to keep it from putrefying.

Joseph Stalin, Lenin's successor, perhaps sensing that the fervor attached to Lenin could be harnessed for his own purposes, created the Commission for Immortalization, and the decision was made to preserve Lenin's body until the end of the Soviet state—presumably forever.

Lenin is kept in a glass coffin at Lenin's Mausoleum on Red Square. The only visible parts of his body are his head and his hands. (Stalin was placed in the same tomb upon his death in 1953, but was removed in 1961 by then-Soviet leader Nikita Khrushchev.) Lenin wears a plain suit, and the lower half of his body is covered with a blanket.

Vorbiov and Zbarsky devised a permanent embalming technique: Every eighteen months, Lenin's body is immersed in a glass tub of a solution of glycerol and potassium acetate. The chemicals penetrate his body, and he becomes like any living human insofar as 70 percent of his body is liquid. After he's taken out of the tub, Lenin is wrapped in rubber bandages to prevent leakage. He is then dressed and groomed. Occasionally, a bacterial growth will develop, but it is quickly scrubbed off.

Lenin has remained in his tomb since 1924, except for a brief evacuation to Siberia during World War II when it looked as if the Nazis might take over Moscow. Lenin's tomb is one of Moscow's main tourist attractions. The Soviet state is long gone, having collapsed in 1991, but its father lives on. Sort of.

Q How come pirates wear eye patches?

A Isn't it obvious? It's one more place to put a jewel or gem. Nothing keeps eye contact like the beauty and shimmer of a diamond or ruby, and pirates were all about accessories.

Okay, the real answer is that most pirates didn't have eye patches. Read the biographies of most of the famous pirates in history—Blackbeard, Bartholomew Roberts, Calico Jack, and others—and you will find that their portraits show them with two patch-free eyes. So the main reason that pirates wear eye patches is because the creators of fictional pirates like them that way. Patches have become an instantly recognizable part of pirate lore, largely because pirates are portrayed as wearing them in movies and books. But that's not to say no pirate ever wore an eye patch. The primary reason anyone wears an eye patch—because he or she has a missing or injured eye—is a plausible explanation for why a pirate would wear one. Swashbuckling, after all, is an extremely dangerous activity.

Another, more fascinating theory involves a "trick of the trade" for all seamen, as well as for law-enforcement officers and armed forces. An eye patch (or simply closing one eye, which doesn't look nearly as cool) can help your eyesight when moving from a bright place into a dark one. For example, say you're a pirate and you've just boarded a ship at noon on a beautiful sunny day. If you're not wearing an eye patch and everyone you need to steal from is below deck, you could be compromised because your eyes have to become accustomed to the dark interior.

Not so with an eye patch! A patch gives you one eye that is already used to the dark. So when you get down below, you simply move the patch from one eye to the other. This allows for much more efficient pillaging.

In fact, you can use this trick the next time you go to see a pirate-themed movie: Close one eye while you're walking through the lobby, and then open it after you are in the theater. Call yourself a pirate, and find yourself a seat in the dark.

Q How did crossword puzzles get started?

A They debuted as "word-cross" puzzles in December 1913. Arthur Wynne invented the first batch, which had no black squares. Three weeks after the first puzzle appeared in the *New York World*, a typesetter accidentally reversed the name, and "word-cross" became "cross word." Everyone liked the change.

Wynne edited the "Fun" section of the *New York World*. Born in Liverpool in 1862, he emigrated to the United States in 1905 and retired from the newspaper business five years after inventing the crossword puzzle. The *New York World* newspaper folded in 1931, and Wynne died in 1945. End of story? Not quite.

Wynne's contribution to American culture became a phenomenon. Dozens of newspapers constructed and ran their own weekly puzzles. By the early 1920s, crosswords were popular in Great Britain, Germany, France, and Russia.

In 1924, two New York entrepreneurs saw an opportunity. The story is that Richard Simon's aunt loved crossword puzzles and asked her nephew to find her a book of them. He couldn't, so he formed a company with partner Max Schuster and published the first crossword puzzle book. They printed 3,600 books on the first go-round, and America went crossword crazy. Simon & Schuster reprinted and sold more than a quarter-million copies in the first year, and their upstart company is now one of the largest publishing houses in the world.

Q How come people get carsick?

A If you're reading this in a car, the answer will get weirdly metaphysical. In fact, if you're reading this in a car, there's a fair chance that you're feeling quite ill right now. This is called motion sickness. Car sickness is just the term for motion sickness that occurs when you happen to be in a car. When you're on a plane, the same symptoms are called airsickness. Sailors can get seasick, and astronauts can be afflicted with space sickness. If you're playing a video game, it's called simulator sickness.

Here's what's happening. We don't just detect motion with our eyes; our peepers notice things that are moving around us, sure, but we also use our inner ears. When our head moves, the gear in our inner ear (or "bony labyrinth," which is a much more enjoyable phrase) tells the brain what's happening.

Say you're reading this in a car and feeling ill. It is believed that this is happening because your brain is receiving conflicting messages from its motion detectors. Your eyes are focused on this page and the words aren't moving, so the eyes are telling the brain, "We're not moving." But the motion detectors in the bony labyrinth are telling the brain, "We are moving because our head is bouncing around."

Let's face it—the brain has a lot of work to do and is understandably vexed by these two conflicting reports. But why do you feel sick? One theory is that the brain thinks the body has been poisoned and that either the eyes or ears are hallucinating, so it starts up the vomit routine in order to get rid of any ingested toxins.

Some possible remedies? Close your eyes to eliminate the conflict. Sit in the front seat of the car and focus on the horizon—this ensures that your eyes see the motion that your body feels. Take some anti-nausea medicine. And for goodness sake, put down this book and read it at home!

Q How come we don't ride zebras?

A What's black, white, and red? A zebra enraged at the thought of someone riding on its back.

While the zebra belongs to the horse family, it is kind of like the deranged cousin nobody likes: He gets invited to Thanksgiving out of a sense of familial obligation, but everybody hopes he'll have other plans. It's inevitable that he'll have a few too many drinks, get all emotional, and then start an argument that leaves everyone avoiding eye contact and thinking up lame excuses for going home early.

Domesticating a zebra is a dicey proposition, though it's been done. For example, it's a real zebra that Hayden Panettiere rides in the 2005 movie *Racing Stripes*, which is about a zebra that aspires to be a racehorse. But the average zebra is far more temperamental than a horse. Zebras spook easily, and they can be exceptionally irritable, especially as they get older. One zebra trainer compared riding the ill-humored beast to "riding a coiled spring."

There have been attempts to create zebra hybrids, such as a "zorse" (a cross between a zebra and a horse) or a "zonkey" (a cross between a zebra and a donkey). But because zebras don't have any particularly useful qualities, such as speed or strength, these hybrids don't have real-world utility beyond the chuckles their whimsical names might elicit.

If you really have a strong urge to "ride a zebra," your best bet might be to head down to the local high school and harass the referees at the football and basketball games. Those zebras may be just as temperamental as the real ones, but they're less likely to kick you in the face.

Q How come they sterilize the needle before a lethal injection?

A The United States is a nation that's terrified of germs. Inundated by media reports of flu pandemics, new strains of drug-resistant tuberculosis, untreatable "superbugs," and mysterious flesh-eating bacteria, Americans put paper on toilet seats, push disinfected carts at the grocery store, and buy millions of dollars' worth of antibacterial hand gel each year. Americans also, for some reason, sterilize needles before lethally injecting condemned prisoners. Seems a little overboard, doesn't it?

Actually, there are many reasons for the use of sterilized needles in lethal injections, the most obvious being to protect the lethal injector. A slip of the hand, an inadvertent twitch, a poorly timed sneeze—one can imagine a number of scenarios in which the needle might go astray.

Indeed, the history of capital punishment in the United States is littered with bungled executions that would be amusing if they weren't so disturbing. Poison gas has been improperly administered, needles have shot from veins mid-injection, and in more than one case, the heads of electrocuted inmates have burst into flames. By far the largest number of botched executions has come via lethal injection, though usually the biggest problem is finding a suitable vein in which to insert the needle (as a number of death-row inmates are habitual drug users).

A second reason for sterilization is the rare possibility (though perhaps less rare now, in the age of DNA evidence) that the criminal could be exonerated or earn a stay of execution at the very last moment—perhaps even after the needle has been inserted. We can hear you now: "Oh, come on! That would never happen!" *Au contraire*. Consider the case of James Autry, convicted of the April 1980 murder of two people at a convenience store in Texas. In October 1983, Autry's turn on the lethal injection gurney (doesn't quite have the same grim ring as the electric chair, does it?) finally came. He was strapped down and the IV was inserted into his vein. Onlookers leaned forward in anticipation. Suddenly, just as the sodium thiopental was about to be administered, the proceedings were interrupted with word that Autry had been granted a stay of execution by a Supreme Court judge, and Autry was unhooked.

Sounds like the stuff of Hollywood, doesn't it? Not really. In March 1984, Autry was executed anyway. It was Texas, after all.

Q How do you make a citizen's arrest?

A Nearly every state allows an ordinary person to make a citizen's arrest, but this doesn't mean that you should convert your garage into a jail and start rounding up suspected criminals. Perp-busting is best left to professionals.

The concept of a citizen's arrest dates to medieval England, where it was standard practice for ordinary people to help maintain order by apprehending and detaining anyone who was observed committing a crime. This remained part of English common law, and over the years, the concept spread to other countries. Standards of exactly what citizens could and couldn't do to detain suspected criminals were modified over the years, as well.

Today, laws governing citizen's arrests vary from country to country; in the U.S., they vary from state to state. The intent is to give citizens the power to stop someone from inflicting harm when there's no time to wait for authorities. It's considered a last resort and is only meant for dire emergencies.

Every state except North Carolina explicitly grants citizens (and, generally, other residents) the power to arrest someone who is seen committing a felony. Some states extend this to allow a citizen's arrest when the citizen has probable cause to believe that someone has committed a felony.

"Arrest" in this context means stopping and detaining the suspect until law enforcement arrives. Kentucky law kicks it up a notch—it grants citizens the right to use deadly force to stop a fleeing suspected felon.

The general guidelines for a citizen's arrest in the United States break down like this: In most cases, you can arrest someone during or immediately following the commission of a criminal act. First, you tell the suspect to stop what he or she is doing, and then you announce that you're making a citizen's arrest. As long as the suspect stays put, you don't have the right to physically restrain him or her.

Don't notify the suspect of his or her constitutional rights; this would be considered impersonating an officer. Typically, you don't have the right to search or interrogate a suspect, either. If the suspect resists, you have the right to use enough force to detain him or her until law enforcement arrives. It's illegal to use excessive force or to imprison someone extendedly if either is due to your failure to notify law enforcement immediately.

Even if you follow the law to the letter, making a citizen's arrest is risky business because, among other reasons, the law doesn't grant you the same legal protection it gives a police officer. In most cases, the suspect could sue you personally for false arrest or false imprisonment, especially if he or she ends up being acquitted of the charges. In other words, if you see a fishy-looking character running down the street, think twice before you spring into action and yell, "Stop!"

Q How do they get stripes in toothpaste?

A Who says we are afraid to delve into the important, life-changing stuff? There are two methods for packaging striped toothpaste, and we boldly plan to tell you about each.

Some manufacturers pump two or three colors of toothpaste into the tube at the same time, side by side. The stripes might come out of the tube a bit messy, since the colors can mix together during squeezing, but for the most part, this method works fine. The paste is thick and packed tightly into the tube, so it won't mix too much.

The other method is to add an extension to the toothpaste nozzle. This extension is basically a plastic straw that extends an inch or so down from the nozzle into the tube. The straw has two small holes on the sides, near the nozzle opening. First, the manufacturer adds a small amount of colored paste into the tube—just enough to surround the straw; then it fills the rest of the tube with white paste and seals the tube at the end.

When you squeeze the end of the tube, the pressure pushes white paste out through the middle of the straw and forces the colored paste through the two smaller holes, adding the colored stripes just before the paste leaves the nozzle. Since the colored paste and white paste don't mix until they are coming out of the tube, everything comes out with perfect stripes.

Does striped toothpaste serve a real purpose? Of course not—it's just a marketing gimmick. Toothpaste includes different ingredients, but they don't need to be different colors or separated. Consumers have the final word on this one, and they have spoken: When Aquafresh came out in the 1970s, it quickly rose to third place in the toothpaste market—thanks, in part, to its pretty stripes.

Q How does the sun make hair lighter but skin darker?

A The key here is a substance called melanin—a bunch of chemicals that combine as a pigment for your skin and hair. In addition to dictating hair and skin colors, melanin protects people from the harmful effects of ultraviolet (UV) light. It does this by converting the energy from UV light to heat, which is relatively harmless. Melanin converts more than 99 percent of this energy, which leaves only a trace amount to mess with your body and cause gnarly problems like skin cancer.

When you head out for a day in the sun and don't put on sunscreen, the sun delivers a massive blast of heat and UV light directly to your skin and hair. The skin reacts to this onslaught by ramping up the production of melanin in order to combat that nasty UV radiation. This is where things get a bit tricky. There are two types of melanin: pheomelanin (which is found in greater abundance in people with lighter skin and hair) and eumelanin (which is found in greater abundance in people with darker skin and hair).

If you're unlucky—that is, if your skin has a lot of pheomelanin—the sun can damage the skin cells, causing a splotchy, reddish sunburn and maybe something worse down the road. After the sunburn, the skin peels to rid itself of all these useless, damaged cells. Then you get blisters and oozing pus, and your skin explodes—no, it ain't pretty. People whose skin has an increased production of eumelanin, on the other hand, are saved from these side effects—the sun simply gives their skin a smooth, dark sheen.

And what's the impact on hair? Well, hair is dead—it's just a clump of protein. By the time hair pokes through the scalp, it doesn't contain any melanin-producing cells. So when the sun damages it by destroying whatever melanin is in it, your mane is pretty much toast—no new melanin can be produced. Consequently, your hair loses its pigment until new, darker strands grow.

The moral of the story? Be sensible in the sun—it's a massive flaming ball of gas, and it doesn't care about your health.

Q How famous do you have to be to go by one name?

A As it turns out, you don't have to be famous at all to go by one name. In fact, the only requirement appears to be a massively inflated sense of your own importance. If you are considering pursuing fame and fortune via the one-word pseudonym, perhaps you can learn from the self-absorbed trailblazers who came before you.

The first thing to know about one-name celebrities is that the overwhelming majority of them are in the music industry. They fall into two categories: those who make up bizarre stage names for themselves (such as Slash, Flea, and Eminem) and those whose real first names are bizarre enough (such as Seal, Madonna, and Jewel).

Regardless of the group to which your celebrity role models belong, they all seem to have one thing in common: They had their pretentious nicknames before they were famous. Gordon Sumner, for example, was calling himself Sting before he joined the rock band The Police. Prince Rogers Nelson's first album, *For You*, bears only his first name, back when most people could have cared less about him. And then you have U2—a band that was nutty enough to have not one, but two single-name members before it recorded an album: Bono and The Edge.

Naturally, there is a certain amount of risk involved in deciding to adopt one name. The last thing you want is to be working as a garbage man and explaining to the customers along your route that they should now refer to you as Shimmer or Justice. Here's a quick tip: If you can't sing or play a musical instrument, it's probably best to stick with the name that your parents gave you.

Q How do bugs know you're about to squish them?

A With some natural aptitude and years of training in an Eastern monastery, you may acquire certain fighting skills that let you drop a grown man to his knees in an instant—but even the most agile martial arts master struggles when it's time to swat a fly. Why? Insects may be tiny and powerless, but they have adaptations that give them an edge against the many larger forms of life that want to do them in.

For starters, the bugs that you most want to squish—flies, cockroaches, and the like—are equipped with compound eyes. A compound eye is a collection of structures called ommatidia. A fly, for example, has four thousand ommatidia in each eye; each ommatidium has its own light-sensing cells and a focusing lens that's positioned for a unique field of view. Collectively, the elements of its compound eyes produce a panoramic vision of the bug's surroundings. The resolution of the resulting image isn't so hot, but it does the trick for detecting sudden movements from almost any direction.

Even when their supercharged vision fails them, insects have other ways to escape your wrath. Many bugs can actually feel the flyswatter approaching thanks to special sensory hairs called setae. When you start your bug-smashing motion, you push air between you and your target. This shift in air pressure stimulates the bug's setae, which signal the brain that something is coming. The movement of the setae gives the bug an idea of where the threat is coming from, and the bug reacts by scurrying in the opposite direction.

It also helps that some bugs are thinking about their getaways before it even seems necessary. In 2008, biologists at the California Institute of Technology used high-speed cameras to observe a group of flies. They found that it takes less than a tenth of a second for a fly to identify a potential threat, plan an escape route, and position its legs for optimal take-off. In other words, when you're sneaking up on a fly and getting ready to strike, that fly has probably already spotted you and is prepared to zip away. This little bit of extra preparation helps pave the way for a Houdini-like escape.

Will the valuable information gleaned from this research enable us to finally gain the upper hand—quite literally—in our ongoing chess match against bugs? Don't count on it.

Q How do dogs remember where they bury their bones?

A Ever watched your dog bury a bone? After covering its treasure with dirt, it'll press its nose into the ground as if it's literally tamping the soil down with its snout. You can always tell when a dog's been digging: Its dirty nose is a dead giveaway.

So how does a dog find its buried treasure weeks or maybe months later? It follows its nose. The enzymes that are released by decomposing bones, especially raw ones, give off a distinctive odor. We can't smell it, but a dog certainly can—dogs can smell one thousand to ten thousand times better than humans can. A dog that's looking for its buried bone will sniff around, keeping its nose to the ground until it finds the exact spot.

Incidentally, this ability to detect decomposing bones is what enables dogs to help law enforcement officials find corpses. According to California's Institute for Canine Forensics, dogs are even used at archaeological digs to locate ancient burial grounds.

A dog's propensity for burying bones is what zoologists call cache behavior. It's also found among wolves, wild dogs, and foxes. When a kill is too large to be devoured at a single sitting, these animals bury what they can't eat in safe places. Canines are highly territorial. Your dog will never bury its bones in another dog's yard, though it may try to sneak in and dig up its neighbor's cache on the sly. Wild canines also bury food in areas that they have marked as their own, which they defend fiercely. During lean times, they will dig up their hidden food stores—it's sort of like having something set aside for the proverbial rainy day.

Do dogs always retrieve the bones they bury? Not necessarily. Cache behavior is an important survival technique for canines in the wild, but well-fed domestic pets may simply have no need for their buried leftovers. Furthermore, cooked bones don't hold the same allure as raw ones—they disintegrate faster, and their scent is sometimes masked by the odors of the surrounding soil.

If your yard is full of holes, you're probably wondering how you can stop your dog from burying bones. Well, the cache instinct is so powerful that there isn't much you can do to deter it. As any experienced dog owner can tell you, a dog will always bury something. If Fido doesn't have a bone, a favorite toy or even an old shoe will do. Indoor dogs often hide their toys under beds or behind sofa cushions. Some veterinarians recommend giving a dog its own sandbox or a pile of pillows where it can "play" at hiding and seeking. These vets add that encouraging cache behavior can be a great interactive way of getting to know your pet better.

So join the fun. Instead of punishing your dog for doing what comes naturally, roll up your sleeves, grab that tattered old stinky sneaker, and dig in.

Q How do we know clams are happy?

A "Happy" is a relative term. What makes you happy may not make someone else happy, and vice versa. And in the case of the clam, happiness is defined thusly: not being dug up, killed, and eaten.

You might be relieved to know that you're not about to be dug up, killed, and eaten—at least as far as we know—but this knowledge probably isn't on your list of things that bring actual happiness into your life. (Besides, you'd have to be in a pretty weird situation to be in danger of being dug up.) For clams, the happiness bar is set pretty low—though what do you expect from a mollusk?

Okay, truthfully, we don't know whether clams are happy. And, really, how much emotion could be experienced by a little hunk of invertebrate flesh surrounded by two equal-size shells? Here's what we do know: "Happy as a clam" is not the whole saying. The whole saying is, "Happy as a clam in the mud at high tide" or "Happy as a clam in the mud at high water."

Clams typically live in shallow water and bury themselves in the mud or sand. So what is it about high tide that would make them happy? At high tide, the water is too deep for clam digging. As a result, clams are protected from people who dig them up and eat them. Maybe they're not "happy" in a way that we understand, but they're at their safest at high tide.

The saying, then, should actually be, "Safe as a clam." But that just doesn't have the same ring, does it?

Q How did Xs and Os become shorthand for hugs and kisses?

A Are you one of those people who signs letters with cutesy Xs and Os to indicate hugs and kisses? Did you ever stop to wonder why you're doing that? What is so cuddly about an X or an O? Much like love itself, the how and why of it remain matters of conjecture.

The X can be traced as far back as the tenth century BC, when it was used as the Paleo-Hebrew letter *Tav* and the symbol of the seal of *Hashem* (God), which stood for truth, completeness, and perfection. During the early Christian era, the X character signified the cross of Calvary (the Latin cross mounted on three steps) and was the first letter in Christ's name (Xristos).

Fast-forward to the Middle Ages, when illiterate people supposedly substituted an X for their signatures. They would then kiss the mark, an act that was comparable to kissing a crucifix or Bible and implied a sworn oath. This practice continued until as recently as one hundred fifty years ago.

According to the *Oxford English Dictionary*, the earliest known use of an X to signify a kiss was in 1763. However, this date is debatable—the practice may have started with handwritten notes, so documentation may be incomplete, which makes it difficult for lexicographers to pin down exact dates and sources.

For our purposes, the origins of the O are even more elusive. In his book *The Joys of Yiddish*, author Leo Rosten wrote that Jewish immigrants in the United States chose O as their signature, as opposed to a cross symbol that represented Christ. Shopkeepers and salespeople also purportedly signed receipts using O. Of course, this explanation does little to solve the hugs-and-kisses riddle.

There is even a running debate about which letter represents hugs and which represents kisses. If you look closely, you will see that the outline of an X can suggest a silhouette of the union of two pairs of lips. Dear Uncle Ezra, an online question-and-answer forum based at Cornell University, posits that the X resembles a single pair of lips pursing for a kiss. Some researchers contend that the X implies a hug because it resembles two pairs of crisscrossing arms. On the other hand, the O could be the hug, as it might represent a pair of arms encircling another person. Or it could be the kiss—use your imagination and you'll see the pouty imprint of a smooch.

Whatever the particulars, Xs and Os should continue to flourish in this era of shorthand text messaging. Unless they are elbowed out by LOL ("lots of love"), of course. To that unthinkable possibility, we say, OMG ("oh my god").

Q How does the clock on your cell phone automatically adjust when you enter a different time zone?

A Your nonstop flight to Chicago takes off from Boston at 7:25 AM. When you touch down at O'Hare Airport two hours and forty-five minutes later, you glance at your cell phone's clock and note that it's only 9:10. You've arrived just in time for your 9:30 meeting. How did your cell phone know Chicago is in the central time zone and automatically set itself back an hour from eastern time in Boston?

Cell phones receive signals from towers on the ground. As you move out of range of one tower, your phone seeks out a connection with another. In Chicago, your cell phone connects to your phone service carrier's nearest tower and receives the correct information from there, automatically updating the time.

However, the system isn't foolproof. If, after you leave your meeting, you rent a car and drive across the state border into Indiana to visit relatives, your cell phone might tell you that you have arrived just in time for lunch at 1:00 PM, but your cousin will say, "Sorry, you missed the tuna casserole." Most of Indiana is in the eastern time zone, so it's 2:00 PM for them and the food is gone. Why didn't your cell phone know that? Because the nearest tower is in Illinois, and your phone is picking up a signal from there.

Techno-geeks are constantly coming up with improvements for automatic time zone adjustments on cell phones and other mobile wireless devices. One of the most recent is a "wireless synchronous time system with solar-powered transceiver," patented in 2008 by a team of six inventors from Primex Inc. in Lake Geneva, Wisconsin.

Perhaps these new solar-powered devices will bring technology full circle. With a few computerized tweaks, we will again be able to use the sun to tell time, just as our ancestors did hundreds of years ago.

Q How many rare diseases are there?

A Most of us are lucky: We weren't born with Hutchinson-Gilford progeria syndrome (HGPS), a disease with symptoms that are similar to premature aging; it leaves, say, a twelve-year-old struggling with the hardened arteries of a seventy-year-old. HGPS is one of the rarest diseases in the world—as of 2008, only forty-some children were known to have it.

What makes a disease rare? In the United States, the National Institutes of Health generally consider a rare disease to be one that affects fewer than two hundred thousand people in the nation. The European Organization for Rare Diseases (EURODIS) defines a rare disease as one that affects fewer than one out of every two thousand individuals in the European Union. In Japan, a disease that affects fewer than fifty thousand people out of the total population is considered rare.

EURODIS states that there are currently between six thousand and eight thousand rare diseases afflicting the human race. What do we know about them? According to some estimates, genetic mutations cause about 80 percent of all rare diseases; most of the remaining 20 percent stem from bacterial or viral infections, allergic reactions, or environmental toxins. But the causes of most rare diseases are poorly understood.

You may have noticed that a lot of stories in the media about rare diseases involve children. It's not just because kids have a lot of heart-tugging appeal. Many rare diseases lead to early mortality, so kids are likely to be the only people who have them. Nearly 75 percent of all those suffering from rare diseases are children; 30 percent of those victims will not live beyond the age of five. Approximately 3 to 4 percent of all children are born with a rare disease, and the number may even be a little higher because many kids receive a wrong diagnosis or, in poor and underdeveloped areas, no diagnosis at all.

What can we do about rare diseases? In 1983, the U.S. Congress passed the Orphan Drug Act, which provides financial incentives for pharmaceutical companies to develop drug-based therapies. As of 2008, the Food and Drug Administration's Office of Orphan Product Development had certified 269 drugs for the market and had given financial incentives for research on more than 1,449 experimental drugs that were in the pipeline. European governments have passed similar legislation to aid researchers.

To raise public awareness, EURODIS, the American National Organization of Rare Disorders, and other similar organizations around the world have designated the last day of February as Rare Disease Day. Every four years, it falls on the "rare" date of February 29, giving leap year special meaning for those who are awaiting something that's even rarer than their disease: a cure.

Q How are old coins taken out of circulation?

A To answer this question, let's track some money from beginning to end. What follows is the tale of Dimey (a dime) and Bill (a dollar bill).

Dimey is one of the nearly fifteen billion coins that was minted at the United States Mints in Philadelphia and Denver in 2007, and Bill is one of the thirty-eight million notes printed in one day during the same year at the Bureau of Engraving and Printing in Washington, D.C., and Fort Worth, Texas.

Off they go to Federal Reserve Banks around the country, excited to be part of $820 billion in circulation. Their journey isn't finished when they get to the Federal Reserve Banks, though. They still have to go to a couple of commercial banks. There they sit and wait, talking about life, the universe, and the latest episode of *American Idol*—until one day someone withdraws them to pay for a new shirt at a dodgy roadside stall. The owner of the stall then spends Dimey on some candy and uses Bill and some of his dollar friends to get into a baseball game. Thus begins a long, adventure-filled journey for both Dimey and Bill. They meet all sorts of people and grow old and worn.

About twenty-one months later—the normal lifespan for a dollar note—Bill winds up in a bank again. The bank manager takes one look at him and dumps him onto the "unfit" pile. After a while, he is packed up and sent to a Reserve Bank. There, he is cruelly replaced with a younger, hipper dollar bill and is destroyed. (About a third of the money that the Reserve Banks receive is declared unfit and is destroyed.)

Tragic, right? It gets worse.

Meanwhile, Dimey is making the rounds. He meets a cute commemorative-dollar coin down someone's sofa, and they have a brief affair before the dollar is dropped into a jar for safekeeping. Dimey is once again sent on his way. About twenty-five years later, Dimey is old and worn, but he still fits into all the machine slots, so he thinks he's just as good as any of the young whippersnapper dimes.

But one day, he ends up at the same bank where Bill was unceremoniously heaved onto the "unfit" pile years earlier. And the same mean bank manager is still in charge. The manager doesn't like the look of Dimey, either, and sends him to a Reserve Bank. From there, he is put into a box with other worn coins. Next to them is a box that is filled with badly damaged coins.

Off they all go back to the Mint, where they see their shiny new replacements heading off to the banks. Then Dimey and his fellow old coins are tipped into a furnace and melted down.

But it's not all doom and gloom for Dimey and company. In the coin equivalent of reincarnation, they're recycled and become parts of new dimes.

Q How fast are you going when you're running amok?

A It's difficult to calculate how fast your head can spin when you're rushing around in such a frenzy. You had better take a chill pill, dude. After all, you don't want to be diagnosed with amok. It's an actual psychiatric condition, which might surprise you since it's used so casually in conversation.

In eighteenth-century Southeast Asia (where the term originated), however, there was nothing casual about it. Studying the etymology of "amok," we find the word had its origins in the Malay *mengamok*, which means "to make a desperate and furious charge." The term was originally used as a noun, and it was meant to denote a Malay tribesman in the midst of a homicidal rage.

Unfortunately, this was something of a common cultural occurrence over there. According to Malay mythology, running amok occurred when the evil tiger spirit (known as the *hantu belian*) entered a person's body and caused him or her to act violently, without conscious awareness.

British explorer Captain James Cook documented his own observations of Malays running amok during his travels to that part of the world in 1770. His records describe frenzied individuals killing and maiming villagers and animals indiscriminately and without apparent cause.

Amok was first classified as a psychiatric illness around 1849, and it's no longer a rare anthropological curiosity confined to primitive Malaysian culture. In modern society, the term (though antiquated) can still be used to describe a mentally unstable individual's homicidal behavior that results in multiple fatalities and injuries.

However, in everyday conversation, running amok is more commonly—and more lightheartedly—synonymous with "going crazy," "going postal," or just "raising hell." And that's in the colloquial and nonviolent sense, thank goodness.

Q How many animals have yet to be discovered?

A Since about 1.3 million animal species around the planet have been identified and named, you might think that we're down to the last few undiscovered critters by now. But according to many biologists, we're probably not even 10 percent of the way there. In fact, experts estimate that the planet holds ten million to one hundred million undiscovered plant and animal species, excluding single-celled organisms like bacteria and algae. This estimate is based on the number of species found in examined environments and on the sizes of the areas we have yet to fully investigate.

The broad span of the estimate shows just how little we know about life on Earth. At the heart of the mystery are the oceans and tropical rain forests. More than 70 percent of the planet is under-water. We know that the oceans teem with life, but we've explored only a small fraction of them. The watery realm is like an entire planet unto itself. Biologists haven't examined much of the tropical rain forests, either, but the regions that they have explored have turned up a dizzying variety of life. It's hard to say exactly how many life forms have yet to be discovered, but the majority probably are small invertebrates (animals without backbones).

Insects make up the vast majority of the animal kingdom. There are about nine hundred thousand known varieties, and this number will probably increase significantly as we further explore the rain forests. Terry Erwin is an influential coleopterist—in other words, a beetle guy—who estimated that the tropics alone could contain thirty million separate insect and arthropod species. This number is based on his examination of forest canopies in South America and Central America, and it suggests that you're on the wrong planet if you hate bugs.

Cataloging all of these critters is slowgoing. It requires special knowledge to distinguish between similar insect species and to identify different ocean species. It also takes real expertise to know which animals are already on the books and which are not. Qualified experts are in short supply, and they have a lot on their plates.

In some respects, time is of the essence. Deforestation and climate change are killing off animal and plant species even before they've been discovered. You may not particularly care about wildlife, but these are big losses. The knowledge gained from some of these undiscovered creatures that are on death row could help to cure diseases and, thus, make the world a better place.

Q How do trick candles stay lit?

A It's unlikely that anyone over the age of three wants to see a trick candle perform its shtick more than a couple of times. Beyond that, it's just annoying. But birthday celebrants of any age might find the science that's involved to be pretty cool.

First, a few words about candles. A candle has two basic parts: an absorbent wick and the paraffin wax that surrounds it. When you light the wick of a conventional candle, the heat melts the wax at the top of the candle. The wick absorbs this liquid wax and pulls it upward to the tip of the wick. The small ember at the top of the wick heats the liquid wax to the point that it vaporizes. The flame ignites this wax gas, creating a bigger flame. So the flame that you see is burning gaseous wax, not the burning wick. As long as there's fuel (candle wax), the process is self-perpetuating: The heat from the flame melts the wax, the burning wick vaporizes the liquid wax, and the flame ignites the gaseous wax.

When you blow out a conventional candle, you extinguish the flame, which interrupts the process. The wick is still lit—you can see a tiny burning ember at the tip—but it only provides enough heat to vaporize the liquid wax it has soaked up. This gaseous wax is what forms the little trail of smoke you see after the flame is gone. The wick is not hot enough to liquefy more wax or ignite the gaseous wax, so the conventional candle eventually goes out completely.

A trick candle has an extra ingredient in the wick that keeps the cycle going: magnesium, which has a very low ignition point. The little bit of heat from the smoldering wick is enough to ignite the magnesium, which combusts in tiny sparks. These sparks then ignite the plume of gaseous wax, and the flame returns. You can see these sparks even when the candle is burning normally; this makes trick candles easy to spot before you try to blow the cursed things out.

To permanently extinguish trick candles, you have to pinch the wicks with wet fingers so that there are no smoldering embers to set off the magnesium. But be careful—this is a potentially painful solution to a pesky problem.

Q How many diapers does a baby go through before being potty-trained?

A The average newborn runs through (no pun intended) about twelve to sixteen diapers per day, according to Diapering Decisions, a supplier of cloth diapers. If we define a newborn as being two weeks old or younger, a baby goes through 168 to 224 diapers in just the first fourteen days of life.

Luckily, the pace slows a bit after that. Between three and six months of age, you'll change a baby ten to twelve times a day; between six and nine months, ten times a day; from nine months to the end of the first year, eight times a day; and up to eighteen months, count on six to eight changes a day.

When will it end?

That depends on your kid. It might be as early as two years; it might take as long as four. WebMD.com says that the average for boys is thirty-eight months; for girls, who seem to do about everything earlier than boys do, the average is thirty-six months.

Thus, you'll change little Georgie between 8,008 and 10,150 times before he's ready to tackle the potty. Little Susan will soil about four hundred fewer diapers; you'll change her between 7,672 and 9,702 times.

If you start the potty-training process early and remain diligent, Georgie and Susan will beat those averages. Good thing, too. With disposable diapers averaging twenty cents apiece, your baby's bottom can drain you of $1.40 per day. If the little bugger does his or her business on the toilet, it's good business for you.

Q How come so many manicurists are Vietnamese?

A No, you're not imagining it. In 2008, 43 percent of manicurists in the United States were Vietnamese. The number was even higher in California—80 percent. What's the deal here?

In 1975, as the government of South Vietnam collapsed, refugee camps for Vietnamese immigrants sprang up all over the United States. More than 125,000 people fled the small country that year, hoping to build better lives in America. Their numbers included businessmen and businesswomen, teachers, and government officials. Most left everything they owned behind, and they had to learn the customs and the language of a new country.

Hope Village was a refugee camp near Sacramento, California, that was visited frequently by actress Tippi Hedren. Remember her from *The Birds*? Well, most of the Vietnamese women at the camp didn't, but they were duly impressed by her beautifully manicured nails.

On one visit to the camp, Hedren brought along her manicurist. The refugees, intrigued by this whole manicure deal, saw an opportunity. Over the next few weeks, Hedren's manicurist taught the women how to do nails. Hedren persuaded a beauticians' school in the area to train the refugees, and she even helped them get jobs. Since a professional manicure in those days cost around sixty dollars, most women treated it as a luxury and didn't have their nails done often. The Vietnamese slashed prices in order to bring in more customers—and the discount nail salon was born.

As the women prospered, their friends and family members—even some males—took up the manicure trade. Since 1975, more than one million Vietnamese immigrants have arrived in the United States, and many of their first jobs have been at nail salons. It's a classic American success story—and it's one that continues to unfold.

Q How come ruins are always underground?

A Ruins actually aren't always underground, but do you think that's going to stop us? We're here to focus on those that are buried, and natural disasters are a perfect place to start. If an earthquake hit or a volcano erupted, an ancient site could be decimated and buried pretty easily, which is what happened to Pompeii.

In Egypt, the powerful desert sands could quite easily have buried something as large as an ancient city. For example, the ancient temple of Abu Simbel was hidden for thousands of years until Giovanni Belzoni dug into the entrance in 1817.

Many sites around the world were abandoned for one reason or another and became overgrown with vegetation. When the vegetation rotted, a layer of soil was formed, and the sites' journeys underground began. Furthermore, archaeologists often search for burial sites, which are underground to begin with.

Really old cities were not exactly constructed with durable materials. In Mesopotamia (modern Iraq), everything was basically made of mud. These mud buildings fell apart quite easily, and the next people who came along simply built on top of the rubble. This went on for ages, until there was a nice thick layer of muddy mush with the occasional surviving piece of detail.

Ancient standards of cleanliness didn't help, either. Rubbish piled up around houses, contributing to the mush. Eventually, people would leave (and really, who could blame them?), and their shoddy mud houses would get reduced to muddy mounds, called tells. Now, archaeologists look for tells and dig down into them. At the bottom of the mounds of dirt, they can often find the remains of buildings, like temples. Temples tended to survive because they were kept clean and in good repair. They often incorporated stone elements into their construction, making them more durable.

Ancient cities that were built mostly of better materials like stone (Rome, for example) tend not to be completely buried. Sure, they're buried a bit, but that's due to the things we mentioned before: growth of vegetation and rubbish piling up. Trouble is, stone robbers came and swiped the ancient rock to make their own buildings, leaving many stone sites in sad statea.

The moral of the story? At least underground ruins are kept safe—until someone discovers them.

Q How do we know cats have nine lives?

A Okay, a cat doesn't really have nine lives—as far as we know, anyway—but it has always been considered a particularly hardy, tenacious, and resilient animal.

Cats were worshiped in ancient Egypt, where the "nine lives" thing may have gotten its legs. In the city of On, priests worshipped Atum-Ra, a sun god who gave life to the gods of air, water, earth, and sky, who in turn created the gods Osiris, Isis, Seth, and Nephthys. Collectively, these gods were called the Ennead—"the Nine." Atum-Ra, who embodied all nine gods (including himself), took the form of a cat when he visited the underworld. So the number nine may have historically come to be associated with cats.

Do cats have an ability to outsmart death? Absolutely—especially when they fall great distances. As a cat plummets, it reaches a nonfatal terminal falling velocity—the friction between itself and the air reduces the acceleration rate to zero. Then, the cat instinctively twists around so that it presents its stomach and becomes like a parachute, with its paws positioned so that it can land on all fours.

In medieval Europe, cats had ample opportunities to test their landing techniques. Unlike in ancient Egypt, cats were treated miserably; during a siege, diseased cats were sometimes thrown over castle walls in hopes that they would infect foes.

The Belgium town of Ypres is famous for its Cloth Hall, which was built in the early fourteenth century to house a thriving textile trade. Cats killed the rats that were destroying the fabric stored in Cloth Hall. But for reasons that may have to do with felines being linked to witchcraft during the era, cats were heaved once a year from the Cloth Hall tower. In modern times, Ypres has turned this long-ago event into an opportunity for tourism. Once every three years, the town hosts a cat festival in which toy cats are chucked from the towers.

Why not use real cats? They would most likely survive. Or at worst, simply use up one of their nine lives.

Q How bad did you have to be to walk the plank?

A You wouldn't necessarily have had to be bad at all. The instigators of plank-walkings—those guys who were brandishing their swords at your back and compelling you along on your fatal journey off the side of the boat—were usually pirates and mutineers. In other words, they were guys who weren't exactly known for their commitment to fairness and justice.

One of the earliest definitions of the phrase "walking the plank" appears in the 1788 book *A Classical Dictionary of the Vulgar Tongue*, which explains it as "a mode of destroying devoted persons or officers in a mutiny on ship-board." The victim was bound and blindfolded and forced to walk on a board that was balanced on the ship's side until he fell into the water. This way, "as the mutineers suppose," they might avoid the penalty for murder. Since no record exists of charges being brought against anyone who forced their officers to walk the plank, maybe those old scalawags were right.

On the other hand, it's possible that plank-walking was an extremely rare occurrence—if it ever really happened at all. In fact, some experts scoff at the notion, saying that the practice existed only in the work of novelists and illustrators. But journalists wrote about it, too. In 1821, a Jamaican newspaper reported that pirates from a schooner had boarded the English ship *Blessing*. When the pirates were unable to get any money out of the *Blessing*'s captain, the lead marauder made him walk the plank. The buccaneers then shot the ousted captain three times as he struggled to stay above the water before musket-whipping the captain's teenage son, pitching him overboard, and setting the entire ship aflame. (Now that's a thorough job!) Another sailor, George Wood, confessed a similar crime to a chaplain just before being hanged for mutiny in 1769. No other documentation exists to validate either story.

Where did the idea of walking the plank originate? It's possible that it was conjured by the pirates who plagued the Mediterranean Sea when it was dominated by the Roman Empire. Yes, there were pirates in those days, and when they captured Roman ships, they would mock the sailors by telling them that they were free to walk home. Of course, at sea, there's no place to walk without sinking like a stone.

But if walking the plank wasn't actually used as a form of maritime punishment, how were unwanted men dealt with at sea? Marooning—leaving a man on a desert island to die—was a popular practice among both pirates and mutineers. In addition, prisoners were tied up and tossed overboard to drown or be eaten by sharks. Eyewitness accounts of hanging, shooting, whipping, and torturing prisoners abound. Fun guys, those pirates.

Q How long can a camel go without water?

A No, they aren't adorable like puppies, kittens, or panda bears. Camels have three eyelids, big lumpy humps on their backs, and are just plain weird-looking. But in the desert, a camel would leave a trail of puppy, kitten, and panda bodies behind—all of them dead from dehydration. So the camel has that going for it.

Camels have a special place to keep water, and it isn't in their humps. Both the Dromedary (one-hump) and the Bactrian (two-hump) camels have oval-shaped red blood cells; the red blood cells in all other mammals are circular. These special oval-shaped red blood cells make blood flow easier when the animal is in a dehydrated state. Additionally, the oval shape allows a camel to drink amazing quantities of water—more than twenty gallons!—in one sitting. Though this much water would send most mammals into shock, a camel's red blood cells can expand to hold the water without rupturing.

Camels also take full advantage of the water in the food they eat. Depending on the plant, they can efficiently use the water contained within, which buys them time before they need a drink. Their kidneys are the kings of kidneys, pulling every nutrient and useful bit from ingested water before turning the leftovers into extremely thick, salty urine.

Additionally, a camel can tolerate extreme fluctuations in body temperature. Humans have fevers when their temperatures rise only one or two degrees above the norm, but a camel is perfectly fine with a body temperature anywhere between 93 and 106 degrees Fahrenheit. This means that a camel can get pretty hot without needing to sweat to cool itself—a characteristic that allows the beast to keep all that precious water inside its body.

The combination of the camel's unique red blood cells, its ability to "take the heat," and its highly efficient kidney and intestinal system enables it to go a week or more without needing water. The actual length of time depends on how hard the camel is working (it can handle hundreds of pounds of weight), how hot the climate is, and how fast it has to move. While a person may live only two or three days without water while riding around on a camel in hundred-degree heat, the camel could live for a week or more.

So here's to the camel—it won't be winning any beauty contests, but it is definitely a front-runner in nature's talent competition.

Q How old do you have to be to die of old age?

A Answering this question is like trying to catch a little ball of mercury rolling around on the floor. It just keeps slipping away.

If we take the question literally, we have to define what "dying of old age" means. For most of us, it's dying at an age when our bodies have become naturally susceptible to maladies than can end a life—primarily cancer and heart disease. When these strike at a certain age, there's less sense of fate having been cruel and unfair to us.

Or we can take the question to simply mean, "How old is old?" In other words, we skip the dying part, which is fine by us. Either way, the answer is slippery.

The definition of "old" has varied by era. In 1900 an American newborn had a life expectancy of fewer than fifty years. Today, it's eighty years or more for a woman and nearly that for a man. In 1950 the life expectancy in India was roughly thirty-two; by 2000 it had doubled. To some extent, the lower life expectancies reflected the higher risk of premature death—from disease or hunger, for example. So it doesn't mean that a fifty-year-old in 1900 was necessarily "old"—although because of poorer nutrition and less advanced medical care (among other important factors), a fifty-year-old back then was typically more enfeebled than one is today.

The fact is, "old age" is an imprecise combination of social and cultural impressions and demographic realities. As U.S. Supreme

Court Justice Potter Stewart said famously of pornography in 1964, "I know it when I see it." So we could say that a person is "old" when he or she is noticeably slowed by the effects of age. The problem is, that and a quarter would have gotten you a cup of coffee in 1980.

So let's discuss some of the attempts to pin a number on old age. In the United States, sixty-five has been the traditional retirement age and when we're referred to as "senior citizens"; for a long time, it was the age when Social Security benefits kicked in. Thus, sixty-five has taken on unofficial status as the beginning of old age—"young-old age," as some gerontologists put it, splitting gray hairs as they go. For them, seventy-five is "old-old," although as people live longer and longer, eighty-five has come to be seen as truly old.

We'll leave it at that—somewhere in the neighborhood of eighty-five—and quote a bit of maudlin poetry, from American writer and businessman Samuel Ullman: "Nobody grows old merely by living a number of years. We grow old by deserting our ideals. Years may wrinkle the skin, but to give up enthusiasm wrinkles the soul."

Q How do you hypnotize someone?

A A hypnotist in a show at a Las Vegas casino might employ a flourish of mystical words and fancy moves to mesmerize volunteers, but it's all for show. The real way to hypnotize someone is much simpler and doesn't require a swinging pocket watch or a lovely sequined assistant.

Psychologists don't fully understand hypnosis, but they generally agree that it's a relaxed, hyper-attentive trance, similar to daydreaming. The defining quality of this state is that subjects don't scrutinize and interpret information as they normally would. When a hypnotist makes a suggestion ("Your hands feel heavy, very heavy"), the subject processes the information as if it was real.

A hypnotist induces this trance by getting a subject to relax fully and focus his or her attention on something. This can be as simple as asking the subject to stare at a blank Post-it note for fifteen minutes or so while saying in a soothing voice that the subject is feeling sleepy and his or her eyelids are getting heavy. Generally, the hypnotist reads from a script or recites memorized lines that help the subject to relax different parts of the body and to imagine a carefree state of mind.

Once the subject is in a trance, the hypnotist can make all sorts of suggestions. How exactly does this work? The hypnotist "programs" specific reactions into the subject—such as, "When I snap my fingers, you will start speaking in gibberish and then you will put a lampshade on your head"—that will be enacted when he or she is summoned from the trance.

Hypnotism doesn't work on everyone. About 10 to 15 percent of the adult population is highly susceptible to it, meaning that these people enter hypnosis easily and respond to many different types of hypnotic suggestions; about 10 percent can't be hypnotized; and the balance of people can be hypnotized but respond in only limited ways to the suggestions. For example, moderately hypnotizable people usually won't follow a suggestion to forget the hypnosis session, whereas the highly hypnotizable will.

For those who are highly suggestible, hypnosis can be an excellent therapeutic tool. It's been effective in reducing nausea from chemotherapy, labor pain, and general anxiety. And if you want to see your friend strut around clucking like a chicken, it can't be beat.

Q How come some bodies of water are salty while others aren't?

A Actually, all bodies of water contain salt. When the salt concentration is high, as in the oceans, it's obvious to the human tongue. In so-called freshwater lakes and rivers, the concentration is much lower—so low that the tongue can't detect it—but the salt is still there.

When oceanographers discuss the salt content (or salinity) of water, they refer to the concentration in terms of parts per thousand. For instance, the saltiest waters in the world—the Red Sea and the Persian Gulf—contain forty pounds of salt for every thousand pounds of water. The major oceans have thirty-five parts per thousand.

In contrast, the Great Lakes—the largest freshwater bodies in the world—contain less than an ounce of salt per thousand pounds of water. Your taste buds would have to be mighty sensitive to be able to pick out a salty taste in these waters.

Bodies of water are saltier in regions with higher temperatures; the higher the mercury rises, the more water is evaporated. When water evaporates, salt is left behind. The evaporated water forms clouds that hover high over land and eventually produce rain. The rainwater drains into a river system and picks up salty minerals from the riverbed. When the river rejoins the ocean, it adds more salt to the already salty waters.

This process is what makes Utah's Great Salt Lake so salty. Numerous rivers and streams empty into the lake, carrying with them the same minerals that contribute to an ocean's salinity. Since the Great Salt Lake has no outlet, the minerals that enter have nowhere else to go. As a result, some sections of the lake have salinity levels that are eight times higher than those of the saltiest oceans. Salinity in the Great Salt Lake ranges from one hundred fifty to one hundred sixty parts per thousand.

You can infer, then, that the saltwater bodies with the lowest salinity would be located in cold regions: the Arctic Ocean, the seas around Antarctica, and the Baltic Sea. The last of these ranges in salinity from five to fifteen parts per thousand. These bodies of water are constantly being diluted by melting ice and continued precipitation, and they evaporate at much slower rates than hotter oceans and seas; they're always getting more water, but rarely more salt.

Drinking saltwater can throw off your body's natural sodium levels, resulting in dehydration. Tap water generally does not have high enough salinity to pose a threat to the average, healthy adult. But the EPA and the American Heart Association have recommended that those who have been instructed to maintain a strict no-salt diet should stay away from water with higher salinity than twenty parts per million. Bottled water has been suggested as a safe alternative, but be sure to check the sodium content on the nutritional label. Even bottled water, it seems, isn't always "fresh."

Q How exactly does someone get into a pickle?

A Well, you'd need a really big pickle—or you'd need to be a really small person. In either case, if you tried to literally get into a pickle, you'd find yourself in a pickle of the metaphorical sort, whether you succeeded or not. Got that? In the non-literal sense, to be in a pickle is to be in a quandary or a troubling situation of some kind. It's obvious that anyone who tried to actually get inside of a pickle would be in a serious mess. But what kind of nut would think of doing this in the first place?

The answer lies in the history of the language. Today when we think of a pickle, we imagine a cucumber that has been soaked in a savory brine—delicious, perhaps, but not much more than a garnish. But before the advent of refrigeration, pickling wasn't just for otherwise tasteless vegetables—it was a way of life. The process creates an acidic environment that kills the microorganisms that destroy fresh food; pickling, then, was an easy way to store scarce food for long periods of time. Before the invention of modern preservation techniques, it was extremely popular to pickle almost anything that was edible, from vegetables to fruit to pieces of meat.

The phrase "in a pickle" goes back hundreds of years to the heyday of pickling. At that time, the word "pickle" referred not only to the pickled food, but also to the pickling solution itself. In fact, "pickle" comes from the Old Dutch word *pekel* ("brine"). And to be in a pickle was to be in the brine—a state of affairs that would have delicious results for a cucumber, but a less pleasant effect on a person. Anyone who has gazed wonderingly at a jar of pickled pigs' feet has an idea of the ultimate consequences.

How old is the idea of being in a pickle? Old enough to have been used by Shakespeare—in fact, he was the first to publish the phrase. In *The Tempest*, Trinculo says to Alonso, "I have been in such a pickle since I saw you last that, I fear me, will never out of my bones: I shall not fear fly-blowing."

We're not sure what kind of freaky stuff Trinculo had in mind, but that's one pickle we're not into.

Q How do pain pills know where the pain is?

A They don't. To explain how pain pills work, we'll use this phrase as an analogy: "If a tree falls in the forest and nobody is there to hear it, does it make a sound?" The idea is that sound is really just waves that travel through the air; without a set of ears nearby to catch these waves—not to mention a brain to process them—they simply remain waves that travel through the air.

Just as you know that you're hearing a sound because your brain tells you that you're hearing a sound, you know that you're in pain because your brain tells you that you're in pain. Your brain is in constant communication with your nervous system; it picks up messages that are sent from nerve endings in all parts of the body. These nerve endings are sensitized to pain by chemicals called prostaglandins. When nerve endings detect pain, they let the brain know about it.

Pain pills such as aspirin, acetaminophen (better known as Tylenol), and ibuprofen (Motrin, Advil, etc.) inhibit your central nervous system from producing prostaglandins all over your body—not just where the pain is. If prostaglandins are canceled out, your nerves don't detect the pain, so they can't tell the brain about it. The cause of the pain is still there, but your nervous system and brain can't "hear" it. You feel better for a time, even though the painkiller isn't actually treating the injury.

So if a tree falls in the forest *and lands on your foot*, both you and the tree will definitely make a sound. If you take a pain pill, however, it will keep your brain from knowing how much your foot hurts...for a while.

Q How far away is the horizon?

A This is a question that can only be answered by doing a bunch of math—the kind of math that many of us were happy to leave behind in college. You need to take into account the radius of the earth, of course. Square roots make an appearance, as do a cosine and a few subscripts and superscripts. Feel a headache coming on?

Even before you do the math, you have to decide what distance you're after. Is it the distance of the straight line from your eyeball to the horizon, or is it the distance you'd have to walk from where you're standing to get to the point that you see on the horizon? Believe it or not, this makes a difference, because the curvature of the earth makes the walking distance farther than the straight-line distance. And the height of the person doing the seeing has a significant impact on the answer, so that has to be factored in, as well. Now our mathematical equation is turning into one of those accursed word problems.

For the sake of simplicity, let's just say we want the straight-line distance. To a six-foot-tall man who is standing in a rowboat on the ocean, the horizon is about three miles away—until he comes to his senses and sits down to avoid capsizing the boat. When he's seated, his view to the horizon is reduced significantly, down to about one mile.

There. That wasn't so bad, was it?

Q How do we know what's in Earth's core?

A The moles aren't talking, so we've had to figure it out the hard way. Geologists say that the center of Earth is a massive metal core. The inner section of the core, which is about 1,500 miles in diameter, is mostly iron and contains some nickel. Surrounding the inner section is a 1,400-mile-thick layer of liquid iron and nickel called the outer core. This core is covered by an extremely hot, slow-moving liquid called the mantle that is 1,800 miles thick; the mantle accounts for the bulk of the planet's mass. Above the mantle is the outer crust, five to thirty miles thick and made up of cool rock, on top of which is where we live and play.

We are familiar with the crust, and we sometimes see evidence of the mantle from volcanic eruptions. Everything we know about the areas below the mantle comes from guesswork and clever remote measurements.

The most useful measurement device is the earthquake. Vibrations from an earthquake generate seismic waves that not only move across the surface of the crust, but also through the planet's interior. Just like light waves, seismic waves change speed as they pass through different types of material. One effect of changing speeds is that the waves refract (turn) at the boundaries between two layers, just as light refracts at the boundary between air and water or as it goes through a lens. Earthquakes produce two types of waves—P waves and S waves—that move through material distinctly and provide seismologists with lots of data.

By noting the time it takes for waves to travel through the planet and observing the patterns of these waves, seismologists have estimated the general densities and locations of different layers of material. The most striking piece of data is a massive "shadow zone" of S waves. Essentially, something in Earth's core blocks S waves that are generated on one side of the planet from reaching the opposite side of the planet.

This suggests that part of Earth's core is liquid, since S waves can move through solid material but not liquid. P waves can move through liquid; their patterns indicate that they encounter an inner solid core after the liquid layer. The intense pressure at the center of the planet apparently prevents the inner core from liquefying.

There's one final piece of the puzzle. All of the planets came from the same swirling mass of matter that formed the solar system. Based on the composition of meteorites left over from this original space junk, scientists have determined the general mix of elements that would have gone into forming Earth. This analysis shows that the planet should include a huge amount of iron, which isn't accounted for in Earth's crust, atmosphere, or mantle. So it must be in the core. As a young Earth was cooling, the heavy iron presumably sank to the center. If only the moles could tell us for certain.

Q How long would it take a pack of piranhas to polish off a cow?

A   The answer to this question hinges on a few factors: How large is the cow? More important, how many fish are there, and how hungry are they? Like sharks, piranhas are drawn to blood; they're killers from the moment they are born. And it's true—a pack of piranhas can indeed strip the flesh from a much larger animal, such as a cow.

The estimated time it would take a school of piranhas to skeleton-ize a cow varies. Some sources claim it wouuld take less than a minute; others say up to five minutes. But marine biologists call these estimates exaggerations. The piranha has a fearsome, tooth-filled grin—but under normal circumstances, it is not considered overly aggressive.

In the United States, the legend of the ravenous piranha began with Theodore Roosevelt's 1913 trip to South America. He re-turned full of stories, many of which concerned the carnivorous fish. It is thought that the Brazilian tour guides who were charged with showing President Roosevelt a good time had a joke at his expense by making piranhas out to be more dangerous than they are. There was an incident in which a cow was lowered into a branch of the Rio Aripuana that was teeming with piranhas, and the outcome was every bit as grisly as legend says. But some vital facts were left out of the story. For one, the cow was sick and bleeding, which spurred the fish into a frenzy. Furthermore, the piranhas were isolated, hungry, and ornery. They saw a meal and went nuts—and we've been talking about it ever since.

Modern jungle-dwellers don't typically see piranhas as a danger. The fish usually feed on small animals—other fish, frogs, and baby caimans. It's not uncommon for a human to be bitten by a piranha, but these wounds are usually small and singular. Little flesh lost, little harm done—the fish and the human go their separate ways.

Of course, this isn't to say that piranhas lack the capacity to wreak havoc. Piranhas are known to be most vicious during the dry season. They are believed to travel in large schools for the purpose of protection, and they stimulate one another at feeding time. In light of this information, there are instances when you don't want to get anywhere near a piranha. If you have an open wound, for instance, it might be a good idea to forego that afternoon dip in the Rio Aripuana.

Q How do smelling salts wake you up?

A Smelling salts were found in many homes in the nineteenth century, thanks to the popularity of tight corsets. From time to time, the extreme constriction caused by a fancy lady's corset would reduce the blood supply to her brain, making her "swoon" (preferably into the arms of a dashing gentleman of means). Everyone would gather to enjoy the dramatic gasp as smelling salts snapped the lady back to consciousness.

Smelling salts are a bottled mix of ammonium carbonate and a small amount of perfume. The ammonia compounds naturally decompose in air at room temperature, so when you take the stopper out of the bottle and place it under someone's nose, ammonia gas floods his or her nostrils. If you have ever smelled ammonia gas, you know that it causes you to gasp, which involves inhaling a lot of air. This can jolt someone back to consciousness after he or she has fainted.

While this undoubtedly is entertaining for onlookers, most doctors today say that using smelling salts isn't the ideal way to revive someone who has fainted. The best approach is to simply let the person lie down for five to ten minutes while the body's blood pressure returns to normal. Loosening tight clothing and applying a wet cloth to the forehead are good ideas, too, but above all, you should keep the person calm and still until he or she naturally regains full consciousness.

It's not as dramatic as a sudden gasp and a look of horror, but it certainly is more pleasant for the swooner—absent a dashing gentleman of means, of course.

 How many licks does it take to get to the center of a Tootsie Pop?

 This truly is a question that has stumped the best and the brightest for years. But now, oh ye of the inquisitive brain, it will finally be put to rest. No more wasted afternoons spent licking your tongue raw, counting in your head, and, in the end, biting down when the candy shell gets thin enough because you just can't wait any longer. Read on and be enlightened.

The question was first posed in a television commercial that hit the air in 1970. An innocent little boy asks a cow, a fox, a turtle, and an owl—none of whom can make it through the Tootsie Pop without biting it. (The owl claims that it's only three, because he licks three times, bites, and the sucker's gone. But we all know the owl is a lying schemer bent on stealing candy from innocent little boys.) The commercial ends on a rather pessimistic note: "How many licks does it take to get to the Tootsie Roll center of a Tootsie Pop? The world may never know."

Well, someone in the advertising industry clearly underestimated the power of human curiosity and ingenuity. In the 1990s, a group of students at Purdue University constructed a licking machine that was modeled after the human tongue for the purpose of finding the answer. After a series of tests, the average number of licks turned out to be 364.

Twenty volunteers from that same group of students took it upon themselves to run the same test with actual human tongues, and they came up with a far lower number: 252. An independent scientist named George Waksman, who undertook the same test on his own in 2006, found that the average number of licks to the center (assuming that the licking was concentrated in a single area) was 253.

For a human tongue, then, it might safely be said that the number of licks to the center of a Tootsie Pop is about two hundred fifty. It should be noted, however, that the number changes drastically based on the size and texture of the tongue, as well as how moist it is and the lengths of the licks. Another factor to consider might be the construction of the sucker itself. If the Tootsie Roll center is not perfectly centered within the pop, it follows that one side of the sucker will be thinner than the other—and, thus, will require fewer licks to wear away.

There it is. If you're satisfied with a broad answer, without qualifications, you can safely say two hundred fifty. But if you desire something more definitive, well, the world may never know.

Q How does El Niño upset weather patterns?

A El Niño, that problem child of climatology, has been blamed for disasters around the world: forest fires in southeast Asia, deadly floods in central Europe, tornadoes in Florida, mudslides in California, droughts in Zimbabwe, and devastating tropical storms in Central America.

What exactly is this atmospheric arch-villain, and where does it come from?

Named, ironically, for the Christ child, the scourge known as El Niño is not so much a single event as it is a predictably unpredictable combination of meteorological conditions that usually arrives in December. The disruptive patterns of El Niño appear roughly once every two to ten years, and to understand what El Niño does, you first have to consider what happens when it doesn't show up.

Ordinarily, during the closing months of the year, trade winds along the equator in the Pacific Ocean blow warm surface water west, forming an immense warm pool northeast of Australia. At the same time, in the east, off the coast of Peru, cooler water rises to replace the warm water that has moved west. The warm pool in the west serves as a weather machine, pumping moisture into the atmosphere that generates storms all around the planet, in generally predictable patterns.

But some years, for reasons unknown to scientists, the trade winds never come. The warm pool never makes it to Australia, and the cool water never rises near Peru. Instead of occupying one spot, the weather machine spreads across a large span of the equatorial Pacific, and its unpredictable location means that the weather that it generates doesn't follow recognizable patterns. This creates a domino effect around the world, forcing a whole slew of atmospheric conditions to follow new, unusual patterns.

It doesn't end there. El Niño has an obstinate little sister, La Niña, that follows El Niño around and behaves just about as badly, but in direct opposition. As the effects of El Niño taper off, the trade winds pick up and blow even harder, pushing more warm water than usual west and pulling up an overabundance of cool water in the east. This turns all of the El Niño weather patterns inside out. Eventually, the trade winds stabilize and conditions around the world return to normal. The cycle is known to meteorologists as El Niño-Southern Oscillation, or ENSO.

It's tempting to blame specific weather events on El Niño, but the truth is that El Niño merely changes weather patterns—lots of other local conditions have to conspire to create an event like a mudslide or a hurricane. It's also tempting, in these days of heightened environmental awareness, to blame El Niño and the havoc it wreaks on global warming. But El Niños have been toying with the world's weather for at least 130,000 years, and while they've grown more frequent in recent times, that trend began some ten thousand years ago.

And as we all know from watching Fred Flintstone, driving a car in the Stone Age did not leave a carbon footprint—just a lot of harmless, three-toed footprints.

Q How does an eel generate electricity?

A At the risk of being particular to the extreme, eels don't generate electricity. The animal commonly known as the electric eel (*Electrophorus electricus*) is actually a member of the Ostariophysi superorder of fish. These critters look like eels, but they reside primarily in fresh waters. True eels, on the other hand, spend most of their lives in the ocean.

Now that we're clear—how does *Electrophorus electricus* create its charge? Bioelectricity!

The electric eel is one of a small group of fish that has an electric organ located in its tail portion, which is most of its body. Within the organ are about six thousand flat cells, called electrocytes, that are arranged in columns, like a stack of plates but with a small amount of fluid between them. These six thousand-some electrocytes are very excitable, electrically speaking, and are not unlike a large group of household batteries serially connected to each other with the positive pole at the head and the negative pole at the tail. They wait for a signal to emit a charge into the surrounding water, and when the electric eel's brain sends the message to "fire!" the electrocytes discharge almost simultaneously in an extraordinarily high-speed domino-like reaction.

In two to three milliseconds, a brief but powerful electric current courses along the eel's body. In that moment, the eel can generate as many as six hundred volts—a jolt five times more powerful than that from a standard wall socket and great enough to seriously injure a human—via rapid-fire, pulsing electric organ discharges (EODs). Mostly electrically inert when not in motion, the electric eel emits twenty to thirty EODs per second when it starts moving and can hit fifty EODs at peak periods.

Why do electric eels emit electricity? Food, protection, and navigation. When it comes to dining, the amount of electricity the electric eel delivers usually won't kill a large fish, but it will stun it for long enough to allow the electric eel to eat in peace, without having to deal with all the thrashing. This electricity also serves to stun would-be predators. Lastly, the electric eel finds its way about its habitat, mainly the Amazon, by emitting EODs that detect objects around it through a process called electrolocation.

Scientists are studying the electric eel and other Ostariophysians, such as the knife fish, to learn more about their production of electricity and the uses we might have for it. So far, however, this has amounted to little more than sideshow attractions. In an aquarium in Japan, for instance, one electric eel helped light a Christmas tree in December 2007. It might seem small—one fish, one string of lights—but the implications of a living, breathing source of energy are pretty fantastic.

Q How come the ancient Romans began their year in March?

A The Romans claimed that Rome's first king, Romulus, came up with the first calendar and that he decided the year would begin on the spring equinox. Most years, this falls on the day we call March 20. Since Rome was supposedly founded in 735 BC, that became year one of the Roman calendar.

We can only guess why the spring equinox was chosen. Maybe it had meaning because the world comes to life again after a cold winter: Flowers bloom, greenery appears, and birds build nests. But there's a problem with that theory: No other European cultures began their year with spring. Some of the ancient Greeks began their year with the summer solstice (June 21); the Celts picked November 1 as New Year's Day; and the Germanic tribes started their year in the dead of winter, much as we do today. Bottom line: We don't know why the Roman year started in springtime.

The original name of March was *Martius*, which was an homage to the god of war, Mars. Romulus designated only ten months for the year, though. Why? Romulus liked the number ten. He organized his administration, his senate, his land, and his military legions into units of ten, so why not his calendar, too? However, ten times thirty or thirty-one (the designated numbers of days of the months back then) made for a pretty short year. Records don't survive to tell us how the people of Rome managed, but within a couple of generations, two more months were added to the calendar.

Did the year continue to start on the spring equinox? Not exactly. Maintaining the calendar was the duty of priestly officials, who could add days when needed. Over the centuries, corrupt priests and politicians manipulated the Roman calendar to extend political terms of office and delay important votes in the assembly—they didn't really give a hoot if it ended up astronomically accurate. The first month of every year was March, but it didn't always correlate to the March that we know—it was sometimes as many as three months off.

Julius Caesar—who was once one of those priestly officials—revised the calendar after he took control of Rome. He brought it more in line with the calendar that we know today; in fact, he even added a leap year. But Caesar's leap year was a little different from ours: Once every four years, February 24 was counted twice. Those wacky Romans.

Q How smart do you have to be to be considered a genius?

A We all know a moron when we see one, but geniuses can be a bit harder to pick out of a lineup.

The simplest gauge of mental capacity is intelligence quotient, or IQ. Different IQ tests use different types of questions, but they all share a basic scoring system, called the Binet Scale (after French psychologist Alfred Binet, who came up with it in the early nineteen hundreds).

In the modern version of the Binet Scale, 100 is the median score, and "average intelligence" is any score between 90 and 109.

Scores of 110 or higher indicate superior intelligence, and scores of 140 or higher mean truly exceptional intelligence—less than 1 percent of the population is in this rarefied category.

In the early twentieth century, researchers who studied intelligence in children began setting a genius benchmark, typically between 130 and 140. They assumed that with this kind of brainpower, these child geniuses would be smart enough to succeed at just about any mental task. The definition caught on with parents and psychologists, and 140 became the most common magic number. So if you crack this barrier, you have a defendable rationale for sporting that "Genius at Work" T-shirt.

But let's not get ahead of ourselves—today, many psychologists believe that IQ in itself is an incomplete, and perhaps even a flawed, measure of intelligence. This is partly because of a concept that was first advanced in 1983, when psychologist Howard Gardner rocked the profession with his theory of multiple intelligences. Gardner posited that people exhibit seven separate types of intelligence: linguistic, logical-mathematical, spatial, musical, bodily-kinesthetic, interpersonal, and intrapersonal. Conventional IQ tests are focused on linguistic and logical-mathematical intelligence. They are, then, a bad measure of other types of intelligence; for example, an IQ test won't reveal artistic or athletic genius.

Another problem with IQ tests, at least where we geniuses are concerned, is that the questions don't measure innovation—the ability to make completely original connections, or what might be called "flashes of genius." Many people with very high IQs end up doing nothing remarkable their whole lives. Does it make sense to call them geniuses, just because they can answer test questions that have established, known answers? As smart as Einstein was, he never would have gone down in history as a genius if he hadn't come up with new ideas.

A more useful, but much more subjective, definition of "genius" is a person with exceptional intelligence (of any sort) that enables him or her to make creative leaps that change how we see or interact with the world. It might be a new way of painting (Picasso's cubism), a new way of explaining natural phenomena (Newton's laws of motion), or an amazing invention (Ron Popeil's Veg-O-Matic).

So, Mr. Smarty Pants, even if you do have a sky-high IQ, don't rest on your laurels. We want to see some brilliant ideas out of you—otherwise, we're taking the T-shirt away.

Q How come bad moods are called "the blues"?

A "The blues" are an abbreviation for the "blue devils." These pesky little demons, popularly believed to bring despondency and sadness, have been haunting minds since at least 1616. One of the first references to them was in *Times' Whistle*, a collection of satirical poems that was published that year: "Alston, whose life hath been accounted evill, And therfore cal'de by many the blew devill."

The glossary for that work contains the following entry for "Devil, blew devill": "'Blue devils,' the 'horrors,' or the remorse which frequently follows an ill course of life." Of course, an ill course of life is what usually transpires when one goes on a few too many benders. (Not that anyone on the Q&A staff would know this in a firsthand way.)

According to John Russell Bartlett's *Dictionary of Americanisms* (1848), "blue" was once a common word in the habitual drinker's lexicon—it was a synonym for "drunk." Interestingly, Bartlett's dictionary also notes that "to have the blue devils is to be dispirited."

Now, you can take "dispirited" to mean "disheartened," "discouraged," "dejected," or "depressed." Or it could mean that someone got wise to your boozehound habits and cleared your cupboards of all spirits (i.e., whiskey, brandy, gin, and rum).

Many early sources, including the 1913 edition of *Webster's Revised Unabridged Dictionary*, define "blue devils" as "apparitions supposed to be seen by persons suffering with delirium tremens; hence, very low spirits." "Delirium tremens" are also known as "the d.t.'s," "the shakes," "seeing pink elephants," or the fevers that creep in during alcohol withdrawal.

Despite the somewhat demonic and alcohol-based origins of the blues, you certainly don't have to be a lush to come down with a case of them. These days, you've got plenty of reasons to have the blues: global warming, a sputtering economy, war and pain the world over. Or, as Ella Fitzgerald sang, you can get the blues because your "ever-loving baby left town."

But it's not all doom and gloom if you're suffering from a particularly nasty case of the blues—they make really good antidepressants now.

Q How do they salt peanuts in the shell?

A No, bioengineers haven't created a super breed of naturally salty peanut plants (yet). The real answer isn't nearly as exciting.

To salt peanuts while they're still in the shell, food manufacturers soak them in brine (salty water). In one typical approach, the first step is to treat the peanuts with a wetting agent—a chemical compound that reduces surface tension in water, making it penetrate the shell more readily. Next, the peanuts are placed into an enclosed metal basket and immersed in an airtight pressure vessel that is filled with brine. The pressure vessel is then depressurized to drive air out of the peanut shells and suck in saltwater.

Peanuts may go through several rounds of pressurization and depressurization. Once the peanuts are suitably salty, they are rinsed with clean water and spun on a centrifuge in order to get rid of the bulk of the water. Finally, they are popped into an oven so that the drying process can be completed.

Now, if they could just figure out how to cram some chocolate into those peanuts.

Q How does scratching relieve itching?

 The urge to scratch is ancient and universal. Who among us has not sighed with relieved satisfaction as a set of nails repeatedly raked down our backs? On the surface, the call-and-response relationship of the itch and the scratch is relatively simple, but there have been some recent scientific discoveries that show there's more to it than just irritation and relief.

Scratching is first and foremost a diversionary tactic. By scratching, you're causing yourself a small amount of pain. This pain diverts the brain's attention away from the itch for a short time. As the pain fades, the itch returns. This is why hospital patients who are dosed with painkillers often report feeling intense itching sensations: You can't effectively scratch an itch if you can't feel any pain.

Most itches are caused by skin irritation. They're the body's way of saying that something's not right. When a bug lands on you, for example, your skin registers an itchy sensation so that you'll scratch the itch and shoo the bug away before it bites you. Irritation also can come from dry skin or harsh enzymes that are absorbed by the skin, as is the case with mosquito bites or poison ivy.

On the other hand, chronic itch—a common disorder that disrupts sleep and can cause embarrassing inflammation of the skin—is not caused by a single external irritant: Its causes are usually internal, stemming from disease or from psychological instability.

While scientists may not know for sure why some itches occur, a study conducted by a dermatologist at Wake Forest University Baptist Medical Center and published in January 2008 has gone a long way toward explaining why scratching brings on such intense relief. By studying the brain's reaction to scratching, scientists have determined that the action itself causes decreased activity in areas of the brain devoted to bad memories and unpleasant sensations.

So scratching can be a kind of therapy; if an itch is purely psychological, then scratching provides a measure of mental relief.

As good as it might feel, scratching is highly discouraged by dermatologists because it can damage the skin. They recommend cold creams and antihistamine drugs to take care of the itches caused by physical irritants. And if you need psychological relief, you can always try asking a therapist to apply the cream for you.

Q How come a dog walks in a circle before lying down?

A Inside every dog is a wolf. Whether the dog is big or small, vicious or just-as-sweet-as-can-be—it doesn't matter. These are animals that are descended from wolves, and somewhere in the recesses of their DNA, certain behaviors are encoded and may never peter out. Turning around before lying down is thought to be one.

Dog experts believe that canines walk in circles before lying down because they're unconsciously recalling the nights their ancestors spent in the wilderness. Wolves don't have the luxury of sleeping on a quilted pad or at the foot of a kind master's bed; they sleep whenever and wherever the impulse takes them. This might be in an area overgrown with tough grasses, ferns, and other plants, so they make a few circles in order to trample the undergrowth. It may not be as comfortable as a plush carpet or a padded area rug, but at least the wolf can ensure that it won't get poked in the rear end by a sharp stem.

Another plausible explanation along the same line has to do with creepy-crawlies. In the wilderness, there's a chance that a snake or an equally unpleasant creature will have already settled into the spot that a wolf has chosen for its nap. The circling may be intended to flush out such critters.

Sure, Fido isn't going to encounter any snakes at the foot of your bed—but old habits seem to die hard.

Q How did black become the color of mourning?

A It's not clear whether black's negative connotations caused it to become associated with mourning, or if its link to mourning caused it to take on those connotations. What is quite evident is that black's history as the color of mourning is a long one.

The relationship goes back at least as far as the ancient Egyptians. The Roman Empire followed suit, and in later centuries the Roman Catholic Church's color sequence assigned black as a symbol of mourning. Indeed, this somber function feels natural. We seem to instinctively associate black with negativity—think of the dark feelings brought on by the passing of a loved one.

Black, however, isn't inexorably linked to doom and gloom in every society. Asian and some Slavic cultures consider white to be the color of mourning. In Buddhism, white is symbolic of old age and death. Brides in Japan wear white, but in contrast with Western culture, where bridal white is a symbol of purity or joy, a

Japanese bride's white robe signifies her "death" from life at home with her parents.

Q How come we kiss under the mistletoe?

A Kissing under mistletoe is meant to bring good luck and prosperity to those who are locking lips. It's a custom that might date back as far as AD 800, and originates from Norse folklore.

The legend holds that Balder the Good, the most beloved of the Norse gods, was killed at the hand of Hother (his blind brother). His weapon? A sprig of mistletoe. Balder was then brought back from the dead through the power of gifts that were showered upon his grave during the season of peace and goodwill. As a show of her gratitude, his mother, Frigg, hung mistletoe and kissed every person who walked under it, which reversed the plant's bad reputation.

Even earlier, around 200 BC, mistletoe was considered sacred in Norse culture. Druids, who were the polytheistic holy people for the Norse, thought mistletoe could cure diseases, improve fertility, and protect against black magic and evil forces. Druid priests, using golden sickles, ceremonially cut mistletoe branches from the oak trees (also considered holy) on which they grew and distributed them to be hung over doorways for protection. Mistletoe was believed to be so powerful that when enemies encountered each other under it, they were to put down their weapons and call a truce until the next day.

The Scandinavians, including the Danish, Norwegians, and Swedish—all descendants of the Norse—continued the belief that mistletoe was a plant of peace. People who were quarreling or couples who were at odds were to declare a truce when standing under mistletoe—and a kiss was the symbol of the truce. The Swedish were among the first Europeans to make their way to North America in the early seventeenth century, and they brought this custom with them.

The traditional practice goes along these lines: Mistletoe is hung over a doorway. When two people of the opposite sex pass under it together, they are to kiss. The man then picks a berry from the sprig; when the branch is bare, no more kissing is to take place under that particular branch.

It is also said that if an unmarried woman passes under mistletoe without kissing, she will remain unwed for the whole of the following year; meanwhile, if a man and a women who are in love kiss under mistletoe, they will get married in the coming year. Another tradition involves burning mistletoe by the end of Christmas season (February 2). If the mistletoe isn't burned by then, all the people who kissed beneath it will become enemies.

Q How do 3D glasses work?

A Three-dimensional—or 3D—glasses have come a long way since they were introduced in the 1950s. Back then, they were used mostly for comic books. Without the glasses, the comics were a blur of red, black, and blue lines. But once you put on the special 3D glasses (usually just thin, colored lenses in a dorky paper frame), the scene seemed to pop off the page...sort of. Characters had increased depth, and debris from explosions seemed slightly in front of or behind other chunks—but by and large, getting the glasses to stay on your face was more hassle than it was worth.

These days, it's much easier to employ 3D technology, and that technology is much more effective. The glasses are cheaper to produce and work better, so more complicated images are being converted into 3D. But while the materials used to create 3D images may have gotten more sophisticated throughout the years, the basic techniques behind them have remained the same.

Three-dimensional imaging relies on the ever-so-slightly different perspectives we see from each of our eyes. Since our eyes are two inches apart, we have what is called binocular vision. A clever illustrator can use this to produce a 3D image. Here's how it works: A 3D image is created in two separate layers. The first layer of the image is shifted slightly to one side and is colored a certain way, according to the filter that is to be used on the left lens of the 3D glasses. For the second layer, the same image is shifted to the other side and the colors are adjusted for the right lens. The resulting image looks blurry and distorted without the glasses, but once you put them on, the image comes to life, showing objects in full 3D.

The 3D effect is produced by the interaction between your eyes, the filters in the glasses, and the specially crafted layers of the image. Most often, the right lens filters out red-colored parts of the image and the left lens filters out the green- and blue-tinted portions. When everything is done in the proper balance, truly stunning effects are achieved, from dynamic explosions to intensely realistic reproductions of the Grand Canyon. NASA has even gotten in on the act, producing 3D images of the surface of Mars. So even if you've never been to the Red Planet—and who has?— you can get a surprisingly accurate idea of what it looks like, thanks to 3D imaging.

As for making the glasses themselves look less nerdy—well, that remains a work in progress.

Q How long is a day on Mars?

A The Martian solar day lasts about twenty-four hours and forty minutes. That's not much longer than a day on Earth, but it would give Earthlings who might eventually colonize the red planet a substantial advantage. Think about how much more you could accomplish with an extra forty minutes per day. It would amount to about an extra twenty hours per month, which ain't chump change.

Those colonists would need to adjust their calendars as well as their clocks. A year on Mars is about 687 Earth days. This is because Mars has a much longer path of orbit around the sun. Earth zips around the sun almost twice before Mars completes one full circuit.

Because of its extended path of orbit, Mars experiences four seasons that last twice as long as those on Earth. Spring and summer are almost two hundred days each; fall and winter are about one hundred fifty days each. Martian farmers would have a lot of time to plant and harvest, but they'd also have to conserve that harvest through a much longer, much harsher winter.

Everything lasts longer on Mars than on Earth. For those colonists, the Martian work week would be an extra three hours and twenty minutes, and the weekend would be extended by an hour and twenty minutes. Summer vacation would be long, but the school year would be longer still.

A blessing or a curse? Depends on what you're doing with your extra forty minutes per day.

Q How come bubble gum doesn't dissolve in your mouth?

A Gum manufacturers try to keep their recipes top secret, but the Wrigley Company acknowledges that most gum is made from four basic components: sweeteners, softeners, flavorings, and gum base.

Those first three categories include ingredients such as sugar, corn syrup, aspartame, glycerin, vegetable oil, and natural and artificial flavorings such as spearmint or cotton candy. These ingredients are all soluble, meaning your saliva will dissolve them as you chew.

This is where the fourth component—gum base—comes in. The gum base stands up to your saliva and maintains its integrity as you grind it between your teeth or blow it into a bubble. Historically, gum base was tapped from natural sources like sorva, jelutong, and chicle, the sap from sapodilla trees.

Today, those natural sources run pretty scarce, so scientists have developed synthetic gum-base materials. Natural or unnatural, gum base does not disintegrate in your mouth.

Why? Because it's essentially a form of rubber. Think of chewing on a rubber band, super ball, pencil eraser, or car tire. None of these will dissolve in your mouth either. (Please, take our word on this!)

Of course, a piece of bubble gum tastes a lot better than an old yellow raincoat, and it's much easier to chew. This is because the rubber in gum base is softer and smoother than normal rubber, and it unites the other, more delicious ingredients. When you chew on it, the flavors of "gushing grape" and "strawberry splash" are released into your mouth, though they don't last long.

And if you swallow a wad of chewing gum? It will come out your other end in one whole piece. And it won't take seven years to digest, as urban legend suggests. It'll run through your system in just a few days.

Q How does salt make you thirsty?

 Table salt contains an essential nutrient: sodium. If you want to keep living, your body must have it. But a little is all you need—excessive salt consumption can kill you. And we're not talking about a slow death from years of heart disease. If the level of salt in your body is high enough, your kidneys will shut down and you'll die, just like that.

But this kind of salt overdose is more of a theoretical problem than a practical danger. Unless you're a castaway who's drinking seawater, you don't have to worry about instant death by over-salinization. In part, that's because your body is very good at maintaining the balance between sodium and water—and one way it accomplishes this is by commanding you to drink when you're eating those deliciously salty snacks.

But why is the balance of sodium and water so important? As you probably remember from grade school, water makes up an extremely high percentage of the human body. And it's not just sloshing around under your skin like a subterranean lake. It's in the blood that circulates oxygen and nutrients to all of your tissues, and it's in the cells of your body, filling them and giving them their shape, like the air that inflates a balloon.

And that's where salt comes in. Your body uses sodium and other minerals—most notably potassium—to regulate the fluid levels inside and outside of its cells. But if the amount of sodium washing around in your body gets too high, this mechanism breaks down and your cells begin to leach water uncontrollably, shriveling like grapes in the sun. That's why your body demands water when you eat salt.

The command to drink originates in the anterolateral hypothalamus, a region of the brain that will continue to nag until you drink something to offset the excess of sodium in your body. So the next time you're sitting beside a bowl of pretzels, do your anterolateral hypothalamus a favor and get yourself a cold drink to go with them. Keeping your thirst at bay is all a matter of maintaining your body's natural balance.

Q How come your stomach growls when you're hungry?

A Did you skip breakfast? No wonder your tummy is growling mad. Those gurgly sounds are technically called *borborygmi* (pronounced BOR-boh-RIG-mee). That's a word the ancient Greeks came up with, and it does a great job of expressing what a stomach growl might actually sound like in spoken form. Go ahead, say it out loud. In case you also skipped English class, it's what academics refer to as onomatopoeia.

But back to your grumbling gut. What's the source of all that clamor? When you haven't eaten for a while, your stomach produces hormones that stimulate local nerves to send a message to the hypothalamus part of your brain. Basically, this is like the hunger light in your head switching from red to green.

In turn, your brain sends a signal back down to the stomach that says, "Okay, then, get ready to eat!" The result? Muscular activity, and a flow of acids and other digestive fluids in your stomach and intestines. And that's exactly what you're hearing amid all your embarrassment. Your stomach is getting juiced up to chow down.

Amazingly, this connection between your brain and digestive system is so automatic that sometimes the mere thought of food is enough to stir up a snarl. (That's why you shouldn't watch the Food Network at night.) But truth be told, stomach growling can happen at any time, whether you're hungry or not.

Often, the sound is simply a sign of your digestive system at work: muscle contractions and digestive juices churning your last meal into a gooey mix and moving it down the intestinal path. It just so happens that the rumble of your tummy track gets a lot louder when there's not much in there to act as a muffler. So don't ever go to study hall—or a silent movie—without eating first.

Q How is it that Friday the thirteenth is unlucky?

A It's perhaps the most pervasive superstition in North America, Western Europe, and Australia. In fact, if you're like lots of other fearful folks, you won't take a flight, get married, sign a contract, or even leave your house on this most doomed of days.

What exactly makes Friday the thirteenth more luckless than, say, Tuesday the fifth? The answer is deeply rooted in biblical, mythological, and historical events.

Friday and the number thirteen have been independently sinister since ancient times—maybe since the dawn of humans. Many biblical scholars say that Eve tempted Adam with the forbidden apple on a Friday. Traditional teachings also tell us that the Great Flood began on a Friday, the Temple of Solomon was destroyed on a Friday, and Abel was slain by Cain on a Friday.

For Christians, Friday and the number thirteen are of the utmost significance. Christ was crucified on Friday, and thirteen is the number of people who were present at the Last Supper. Judas, the disciple who betrayed Jesus, was the thirteenth member of the party to arrive.

Groups of thirteen may be one of the earliest and most concrete taboos associated with the number. It's believed that both the ancient Vikings and Hindus thought it unpropitious to have thirteen people gather together in one place. Up until recently, French socialites known as *quatorziens* (fourteeners) made themselves available as fourteenth guests to spare dinner parties from ominous ends.

Some trace the infamy of the number thirteen back to ancient Norse culture. According to mythology, twelve gods had arrived to a banquet, when in walked an uninvited thirteenth guest—Loki, the god of mischief. Loki tricked the blind god Hother into throwing a spear of mistletoe at Balder, the beloved god of light. Balder fell dead, and the whole Earth turned dark.

In modern times, thirteen continues to be a number to avoid. About 80 percent of high-rise buildings don't have a thirteenth floor, many airports skip gate number thirteen, and you won't find a room thirteen in some hospitals and hotels.

How did Friday and thirteen become forever linked as the most disquieting day on the calendar? It just may be that Friday was unlucky and thirteen was unlucky, so a combination of the two was simply a double jinx. However, one theory holds that all this superstition came not as a result of convergent taboos, but of a single historical event.

On Friday, October 13, 1307, King Philip IV of France ordered the arrest of the revered Knights Templars. Tortured and forced to confess to false charges of heresy, blasphemy, and wrongdoing, hundreds of knights were burned at the stake. It's said that sympathizers of the Templars then condemned Friday the thirteenth as the most evil of days.

No one has been able to document if this eerie tale is indeed the origin of the Friday the thirteenth superstition. And really, some scholars are convinced that it's nothing more than a phenomenon created by twentieth-century media. So sufferers of paraskevidekatriaphobia (a pathological fear of Friday the thirteenth), take some comfort—or at least throw some salt over your shoulder.

Q How can you tell if a man will go bald?

A No thoughtful woman would make a decision about marriage based on something as superficial as future baldness. Nevertheless, when a man is down on bended knee, it's only natural to survey the landscape and ponder the hair forecast.

The safe bet is that your man will go bald ... assuming he lives long enough. According to Medem Medical Library, about 25 percent of men have begun to lose hair by age thirty; around two-thirds have lost hair by sixty; and 85 percent are sporting big old bald spots by age seventy. Typically, baldness begins with a receding hairline at the temples and thinness on the crown of the scalp, and it spreads out from there. And, of course, the earlier it begins, the more severe it's likely to be.

Baldness is hereditary, but the genetics involved are so complicated and mysterious that examining relatives won't help you much in your quest to read the future of your squeeze's follicles. The better approach is to gauge whether significant hair loss is already underway, by actually observing how easily and quickly he's shedding his mane. At any given time, 90 to 95 percent of the hundred thousand follicles on a non-balding man's head are actively growing hair. The follicles go through periods of growth and dormancy, and as old hairs fall out, new ones replace them. But when male pattern baldness is underway, the periods of active hair growth become less frequent, the hairs themselves get shorter and shorter, and the follicles shed the hairs more readily.

When a man isn't going bald, it's normal for him to lose one hundred to two hundred hairs a day. If a man is losing more hair than that, he's probably en route to cue-ball town. Of course, it's not exactly practical to follow your honey around, grabbing and cataloging each hair that unceremoniously falls off his head. Fortunately, researchers at the Baylor College of Medicine in Houston have developed a simpler test. They determined that young men with no signs of male pattern baldness shed about ten hairs when they comb their hair for sixty seconds. More hairs than that could indicate the advent of baldness—though years may pass before the hair loss becomes noticeable.

If you want to be really scientific about it, you can shell out about one hundred fifty dollars for a DNA test. The California company HairDX analyzes genetic samples—it looks for a telltale genetic variant that's shared by 95 percent of men who go bald before old age. If the variant is present, it means a man has a 60 percent chance of going bald by age forty; if a man tests positive for another, less common variant, he has an 85 percent chance of being a cue ball by age forty. The only catch is that you have to swab the inside of the mouth to collect the sample, which isn't the most romantic gesture when your true love has just proposed.

Q How come grown men still need toys?

A Every Christmas, a scene like this one unfolds in households across America: The kids wake up at the crack of dawn. Silently, with anticipation and bated breath, they creep downstairs to see what Santa has left them. They hear noises in the living room—clicks and rasps, a murmur. Is it possible that Santa is still there? They reach the doorway, peek in, and find... Dad, playing with the video game system that was supposed to be for the kids. Come on, Dad!

Of course, it's commonly held wisdom that most men are just big kids at heart. And like kids, they need their toys, whether their playthings are video games, smart-phones, or sports cars. But why is this? After all, everybody knows that the adult world is a sober, stressful place with no room for childish games.

Maybe not. Play theorists (yes, they really exist) suggest that toys and games aid mental development in children and adults alike. For children, games act as staging grounds for the adult world. (They require cognitive skills like understanding rules or strategy, and social skills like cooperation and communication.) But this development doesn't stop at adulthood. According to scientists, playing with toys can help "potentiate novelty." (This is a fancy way of saying that it can inspire creativity, generate new ideas, and help adults approach problems in new ways.) In fact, Albert Einstein himself stated that play is essential to any productive thought. And who's going to argue with him?

But why do men seem more apt to play with toys than women? While the reasons haven't been extensively studied, one explanation may lie in the respective roles that men and women have traditionally played in society. For most of modern history, men have been the wage-earners, the handlers of weighty responsibilities—the very ones for whom "potentiating novelty" is the most important. And as bacon-bringers and novelty-potentiators, they deserve nothing less than a hot meal when they get home from the office, a nice martini, and, obviously, a sixteen-thousand-dollar stereo system. A woman, on the other hand, is trained by society to play the role of caregiver, of homemaker, of nurturer. There is no time—or excuse—for frivolity when the laundry needs washing, the kids need bathing, and the husband's martini needs mixing.

Of course, some people—husbands, mainly—might call this assumption a load of rubbish. After all, isn't an eight-hundred-dollar Prada handbag a type of toy? Regardless, as gender roles continue to evolve, there may be a correlating shift in how men and women approach leisure. And this may be a good thing for everybody because in addition to their sociological importance, toys may also have health benefits.

Being an adult can be stressful—and stress, doctors tell us, is one of the worst things for our bodies. Enter toys. Play therapists suggest that one of the best ways of reducing stress is to hit the arcade or pick up a hobby. In fact, an intense game of air-hockey at that arcade may have health benefits beyond mere stress reduction. Indeed, mounting evidence suggests that active use of the brain—through the creative thinking or puzzle-solving involved with many computer games, for example—may help stave off degenerative brain diseases like Alzheimer's. This is good news for the 53 percent of adults who reported to the Pew Center in 2008 that they routinely play video games.

So go ahead, Dad—it's okay to play a little Xbox on Christmas morning. Just give the kids a turn once in a while.

Q How did the stork get the job of delivering babies?

A It's been the salvation of uptight parents everywhere. Inquisitive little children all eventually arrive at the same brutal question: "Where do babies come from?" The most expedient response? "The stork brings them." But stork folklore goes way beyond lazy parenting. The large, long-necked bird has been associated with maternity and fertility in many cultures for thousands of years.

In Greek mythology, the story of the stork that we know gets turned on its head. Gerana, queen of the Pygmies, angers the goddess Hera and is changed into a stork. She then tries to steal her own child away but is constantly foiled by other family members. Early Christians believed the stork to be a symbol of marital chastity. In Norse mythology, the stork represents a commitment to family, based on the (erroneous) belief that storks are monogamous. The Hebrew word for stork means "kind mother."

The myth of the stork delivering babies appears to have taken hold in Europe, in places such as Holland, Germany, and Poland, where the migratory birds arrived for breeding about nine months after midsummer—during springtime, just as all the babies who were conceived during the lusty fun of midsummer festivals were being born. A stork nesting on the roof at the same time that a new baby arrived was seen as much more than a coincidence, so storks came to be associated with the welcome addition of little blessings in a home. In the hyper-prudish Victorian era, this stork/baby association provided a handy way to avoid the embarrassment of discussing childbirth with curious youngsters.

Although the stork remains a common symbol of birth, children today who ask where babies come from are likely to receive a much more progressive response, such as, "Go ask your mother."

Q How does helium make your voice squeaky?

A Everyone loves balloons, especially the ones filled with helium. What's great about helium-filled balloons is not just the cheery way they float along, but also the way the gas inside alters your vocal cords. By inhaling small amounts of helium, a person can change his or her voice from its regular timbre to a squeaky, cartoon-like sound. But how does it work?

The simplest explanation is that since helium is six times less dense than air—the same reason a helium balloon floats—your vocal cords behave slightly differently when they're surrounded by the element. Additionally, the speed of sound is nearly three times faster in helium than in regular air, and this lends quite a bit of squeak to your voice as well.

The opposite reaction can be achieved using a chemical known as sulfur hexafluoride, though it's nowhere near as common as helium and is much more expensive. Whereas helium is readily available in grocery and party stores, sulfur hexafluoride is generally used in electrical power equipment, meaning that one would have to order somewhat large quantities of it from a specially licensed provider. If you do manage to get a hold of some, the results are plenty entertaining: Sulfur hexafluoride drops your voice incredibly low, much like that of a disc jockey or a super villain.

It's important to note, however, that inhaling helium (or other, similar gases) is dangerous. There's a high risk of suffocating, because a person's lungs aren't designed to handle large quantities of helium. What's more, the canisters used to fill balloons contain more than just helium—there are other substances in there that help properly inflate a balloon that can be harmful to your body if they're inhaled. So while a helium-laced voice sounds funny, it actually shouldn't be taken as a joke.

 How come women need so many shoes?

 Where's Imelda Marcos when you need her? The former first lady of the Philippines—and world's best-known shoe collector—reportedly owned 1,220 pairs when she fled the presidential palace in 1986. She would be the perfect source for a definitive answer to this age-old question, but alas, she's probably out prancing through the streets of Manila in expensive size eight-and-a-half Ferragamos.

So instead, let's address why men find this footwear fixation so perplexing in the first place. Men generally wear pants, or some variation thereof, and said pants come in three basic colors: black, navy, and khaki.

You know what that means? No one is going to crane his or her neck to see what Joe is sporting underneath his spiffy cuffed-hem Dockers. And it doesn't matter anyway. Chances are that Joe's shoes are typical leather loafers or lace-up oxfords in a pedestrian shade of black or brown. The heels are unremarkably flat, unless Joe happens to be living in seventeenth-century France or competing in a professional ballroom dancing competition.

Most guys can get by with five pairs of shoes or fewer. These include—and are often limited to—dress shoes for work, athletic shoes for working out, and a pair of scuffs for picking up the Sunday paper. And this is exactly why men don't get why women need so many shoes—the operative word being "need."

You see, modern women are major multitaskers. Shoes take their scurrying feet to work, the gym, day care, the grocery store, the beach, after-school sports, dancing, and swanky dinner parties—all in the span of a week. Yes, it's true that you can wear only one pair of shoes at a time. But if you've ever had a stiletto heel get caught in a muddy sinkhole of damp grass, you know that you simply cannot wear a pair of four-inch Jimmy Choos to the park.

Take a look in a woman's closet and you'll find pants, skirts, shorts, skorts, and dresses of every conceivable color and length. Most of these fashions direct an observer's eye right to a woman's legs and feet—so guess what? The style, heel, and color of her shoes have to be spot-on.

Shoe designers know this, and that's why you find women's shoes with wedge heels, kitten heels, peep toes, Mary Jane straps, and colors like orange patent leather. And it's a good thing, because the busy women of this world clearly need shoes for every outfit, every occasion, and every terrain.

The truth? Men just can't handle that amount of mind-blowing fashion coordination. If they could, they'd be smart enough to own more than one pair of Nikes.

Q How does a compass always point north?

A In the early days of navigation, sailors relied upon the positions of stars and constellations to determine where they were and where they were going. While this worked reasonably well, the development of the compass was a vast improvement.

So how does a compass work, exactly? An early version of the modern magnetic compass was in use in China as early as AD 850, and the more recognizable mariner's compass was developed in Europe around 1190. There have been many advancements in compass technology since its inception, but in its most basic form, a compass is simply a free-spinning magnet above an image of the four cardinal directions. Since a magnet will naturally point north, all you have to do is let the compass dial swing until it comes to rest and then place the "north" part of the image where the needle is.

Of course, this only works because we know that the needle will always point north. The real question, then, is why does it do this? The truth of the matter is that a magnet doesn't only point north—it points north and south, with each end of the magnet pointing toward either the North or South Pole of Earth. Earth's magnetic field attracts the ends of the magnet toward the north and the south, but for simplicity's sake, the north-facing end of the needle is all that is denoted on a compass, usually with red paint.

You might be wondering, "How does one know which end is which, without using a compass?" Quite simply, you can use the position of the sun to calibrate a magnet. As long as you remember that the sun rises in the east and sets in the west, you can determine which end of the magnet is pointing north.

Q How is it that Maine is called "Down East"?

A The state of Maine occupies the northeastern-most corner of the United States. You might think, therefore, that when people in Boston, which is fifty miles to the south, take a jaunt to Maine, they would say they're going "up to Maine" for the summer and returning "down to Boston" when the season is over. Instead, Bostonians, or at least the old-fashioned "proper" ones, will tell you that they're going "down to Maine" and coming back "up to Boston." Say what? Have they lost their compasses?

Not exactly. The phrase "down east" comes from sailors' lingo. Back in the nineteenth century, the fastest way to travel was by clipper ship. Fortunately, a steady wind from the south swept up the East Coast, pushing ships northeast. When sailors travel with the wind at their backs, they say they are traveling downwind. "Down east" means going east with the wind behind you. Returning south, ships would be pushing against the wind, or upwind.

Pretty simple. But in this day and age, when most vacationers arrive by interstate highway, why do Mainers still like to call their state Down East? Maybe it's because people who can stick it out in a land of long, dark winters are pretty darn proud of their history and like to celebrate it in all kinds of unique ways, from choosing the white pine cone as their state "flower" to claiming Moxie as their official state drink. And, of course, nothing's more fun than confusing first-time tourists with friendly signs pointing them north to Down East.

Contributors

Angelique Anacleto specializes in style and beauty writing. She has written for leading salon industry publications and is currently working on a children's book.

Brett Ballantini is a sportswriter who has written for several major sports teams and has authored a book titled *The Wit and Wisdom of Ozzie Guillen*.

Diane Lanzillotta Bobis is a food, fashion, and lifestyle writer from Glenview, Illinois.

Joshua D. Boeringa is a writer living in Mt. Pleasant, Michigan. He has written for magazines and Web sites.

Michelle Burton is a writer and editor with one foot in Chicago and the other in Newport Beach, California. She has written guidebooks and hundreds of feature articles and reviews.

Anthony G. Craine is a contributor to the *Britannica Book of the Year* and has written for magazines including *Inside Sports* and *Ask*. He is a former United Press International bureau chief.

Dan Dalton is a writer and editor who hails from Michigan.

Paul Forrester is an editor living in New York City.

Shanna Freeman is a writer and editor living near Atlanta. She also works in an academic library.

Ed Grabianowski writes about science and nature, history, the automotive industry, and science fiction for Web sites and magazines. He lives in Buffalo, New York.

Jack Greer is a writer living in Chicago.

Tom Harris is a Web project consultant, editor, and writer. He is the cofounder of Explainist.com and was leader of the editorial content team at HowStuffWorks.com.

Vickey Kalambakal is a writer and historian based in Southern California. She writes for textbooks, encyclopedias, magazines, and ezines.

Brett Kyle is a writer living in Draycott, Somerset, England. He also is an actor, musician, singer, and playwright.

Noah Liberman is a Chicago-based sports, entertainment, and business writer who has published two books and has contributed articles to a wide range of newspapers and national magazines.

Letty Livingston is a dating coach and relationship counselor.

Alex Nechas is a writer and editor based in Chicago.

Jessica Royer Ocken is a freelance writer and editor based in Chicago.

Thad Plumley is an award-winning writer who lives in Dublin, Ohio. He is the director of publications and information products for the National Ground Water Association.

ArLynn Leiber Presser is a writer living in suburban Chicago. She has written dozens of books.

Pat Sherman is a writer living in Cambridge, Massachusetts. She is the author several books for children, including *The Sun's Daughter* and *Ben and the Proclamation of Emancipation*.

Carrie Williford is a writer living in Atlanta. She was a contributing writer to HowStuffWorks.com.

Factual verification: Darcy Chadwick, Barbara Cross, Bonny M. Davidson, Andrew Garrett, Cindy Hangartner, Brenda McLean, Carl Miller, Katrina O'Brien, Marilyn Perlberg